Teacher's Galaxy of
Reading Improvement Activities —
with model lesson plans

Teacher's Galaxy of Reading Improvement Activities

-with model lesson plans

Richard A. Thompson
Carlyne Ussery McGregor
Janet R. Thompson

Parker Publishing Company, Inc., West Nyack, N.Y.

Teacher's Galaxy
of Reading Improvement Activities—
with Model Lesson Plans
by Richard A. Thompson,
Cavlyne Ussery McGregor,
and Janet R. Thompson

© 1979, *by*

PARKER PUBLISHING COMPANY, INC.

West Nyack, N.Y.

Library of Congress Cataloging in Publication Data

Thompson, Richard A
    Teacher's galaxy of reading improvement activities--
with model lesson plans.

    Includes index.
    1. Reading (Elementary) 2. Reading (Secondary
education) I. McGregor, Cavlyne Ussery,   joint
author. II. Thompson, Janet R.,   joint author.
III. Title.
LB1573.T493   428'.4'0712   79-11144
ISBN 0-13-888362-9

Printed in the United States of America

To Denise, Dana, and Michael:
I dedicate my efforts in this book to you
because without you my life would be incomplete.

_____

To Carol, David, Tim and Kim:
Our part in this book is dedicated to you
because you give us love and joy,
without which nothing of substance can be accomplished.
With thankfulness,
Mom and Dad

Why This Time-Saving Material Is of Practical Value to You

Most teachers would agree that the teaching of reading skills is at the forefront of skill priorities. Fairly or not, principals and parents form judgments about your total teaching effectiveness on the basis of a few observations. Usually your reading classes are of particular interest to them, and the impression they form of your reading program influences greatly their perception of you as a teacher in all subject areas. Recognizing that the teaching of reading is THE priority skill in most people's minds, you will find *Teacher's Galaxy of Reading Improvement Activities—With Model Lesson Plans* to be an invaluable aid in helping you effectively demonstrate your teaching skill. Not only will these tested lessons materially aid your reading program, but people observing you apply these lessons will be quick to recognize your effectiveness.

This TEACHER'S GALAXY OF READING IMPROVEMENT ACTIVITIES will also help you use your time more efficiently. We *know* how valuable time is to a busy teacher. The writing of objectives and procedures must be done, but it is time-consuming. Think of the time you can save when you have reading lessons available for every reading subskill. You can meet your students' diverse needs without losing hours per week thinking, designing, and writing lesson plans. We have done this for you. For example, you know that several students need consonant blend instruction. By looking under the major division heading of "Sound and Symbol Recognition," you can locate the skill lesson for blends. Your objective is listed; your material needs, if any, are listed; and your precise teaching procedures are there—listed one, two, three. Additionally, follow-up activities are given. Many examples of procedures and activities are provided. Your planning is done. You have saved yourself work and the commodity that is unproducible—time.

For years, evidence has been accumulating that reading instruction is more effective if skill lessons are taught systematically. This involves discovering the skills students lack and systematically providing precise instruction in those areas. To help you provide reading skill instruction on a student need basis, these prescriptive lessons cover all the reading subskills. Whatever diagnostic instrument you use, you will have available precise, instructional lessons to meet specific student needs which are concisely written for your convenience. With these activities, you will be able to meet the individual reading needs of your students.

Now, you can see why this material is *practical*. It makes a valuable contribution to your effectiveness and enables you to meet individual student needs. It assists you in systematizing your instructional procedures, and saves you work and planning time.

Becoming acquainted with the organization of this material will help you perceive its value. Your *Galaxy of Reading Improvement Activities* is divided into these broad reading skill areas: "Prereading Skills," "Vocabulary," "Context Clues," "Literal Comprehension Skills," "Interpretive Comprehension Skills," "Critical Comprehension Skills," and "Study Skills." To elaborate, under the division labeled "Sound and Symbol Recognition," lessons are found for developing skill in recognizing like and unlike vowel sounds, single consonants, blends, and digraphs. Under "Structural Analysis," lessons are provided for teaching inflected word forms, possessives, affixes, prepositional meanings, compound words and other skills. All reading subskills are covered. For example, using *Galaxy* to solve your instructional problems is a simple A B C process. First, turn to the table of contents and locate the skill lesson you need; then proceed to the pages indicated; and finally check the index for related material. Regardless of what grades you are assigned to teach you will be ready to meet your students' individual needs. Should you change grade levels next year, you will be ready for reading instruction.

Reading instruction is going through the most significant change since the introduction of basal readers over a century and a half ago. The change is from programming students through basal readers, under the assumption that the program knows the skill needs of students, to a prescriptive teaching of reading skill needs. Reading instruction today is emerging as a diagnostic-prescriptive-diagnostic process in which teachers are beginning to use reading management systems. Using this kind of instructional scheme requires teachers to focus directly on teaching precise reading skills. *Teacher's Galaxy of Reading Improvement Activities* is just the systematic, well-thought-out reading teacher strategy kit needed to help you meet precisely your students' needs. For those teachers using basal programs, these Activities are ideal for augmenting the teacher manual suggestions. Whether you have your students travel through a reading program or you use a diagnostic-prescriptive approach, your "Galaxy of Lesson Plans" will help you provide effective instruction while minimizing expediture of your planning time.

The authors

Contents

1. **Developing Prereading Skills** **19**

   Auditory Discrimination • 22
   Auditory Memory • 23
   Visual Discrimination • 25
   Visual Memory • 26
   Listening • 28
   Motor Development—Body Control • 29
   Motor Development—Eye-Hand Control • 31
   Oral Language Development • 32
   Left-to-Right Orientation • 34
   Sequence—Pictures • 35
   Sequential Order of Events • 36
   Alphabet Knowledge • 38
   Copying Words • 39

2. **Keys to Vocabulary and Comprehension** **41**

   Synonyms • 43
   Antonyms (Lesson 1) • 48
   Antonyms (Lesson 2) • 49
   Homonyms • 50
   Heteronyms • 52
   Sight Vocabulary • 53
   Multiple Meanings • 54

3. Context Clues for Discovering New Words 57

Using Context Clues (Lesson 1) • 59
Using Context Clues (Lesson 2) • 61
Using Context Clues (Lesson 3) • 62
Homophones in Context • 63
Selecting Correct Synonyms • 64
Recognizing Antonyms in Context • 66
Homographs in Context • 68

4. Teaching Sound and Symbol Recognition (Phonics) 71

Initial Consonants (Single)—Auditory • 74
Initial Consonants (Single)—Visual • 75
Initial Consonants (Single)—Application • 76
Ending Consonants • 77
Consonant Blends (Visual-Auditory) • 79
Consonant Blends (Association and
  Application) • 80
R-Blends • 81
Other Consonant Blends
  (sc, sk, sl, sm, sn, sp, st, sw) • 82
Consonant Digraphs • 86
Short Vowels • 87
Long Vowels • 88
Long and Short Vowels • 89
Silent Vowel Sounds • 90
R-Controlled Vowels • 91
Vowel Combinations • 92
Rhyming Words—Lesson 1 • 93
Rhyming Words—Lesson 2 • 95
Blending Word Elements—Lesson 1 • 96
Blending Word Elements—Lesson 2 • 97
Silent Letters in Words • 98

5. **Increasing Structural Analysis Skills** 101

Inflected Word Ending (s) • 103
Inflected Words: Singular/Plural • 105
Inflected Word Ending (ed) • 106
Inflected Word Ending (ing) • 107
Affixes—Prefixes • 108
Affixes—Suffixes • 108
Possessives (Singular Form) • 109
Possessives (Plural Form) • 111
Adjectival Recognition • 113
Prepositional Phrases • 114
Pronouns • 115
Contractions • 117
Compound Words • 118
Root Words • 122
Verbs: Irregular Agreement with Subject • 123
Verbs: Tense Usage • 124
Nouns and Verbs (Distinguishing Between) • 125
Phrase Meaning • 127
Identification of Sentence Parts • 129
Punctuation: Scrambled Sentences • 130
Quotations • 131
Number of Syllables (Audio-Visual) • 133
VCCV Principle • 134
VCV Principle • 135
Syllables and Vowel Principles • 136

6. **Enlarging Literal Comprehension Skills** 139

Sensible Sequence • 141
Sequence of Events—Parts • 143
Understanding Sequence of Events • 145
Story Setting • 148
Recalling Details (*How* Words) • 150

Recalling Details (*Why* Words) • 151
Recalling Details (*Where* Words) • 152
Recalling Details (*When* Words) • 153
Recalling Details (*Who/What* Words) • 154
Recalling Details (Action Words) • 155

7. How to Improve Interpretive Comprehension Skills 157

Cause and Effect Relationships • 160
Perception of Inference • 161
Drawing Conclusions • 163
Prediction of Future Action by
    Drawing Inferences • 165
Main Idea (Titles) • 165
Main Idea (Details) • 168
Main Idea (Paragraphs) • 169
Character Feelings • 171
Character Analysis Related to
    Character Actions • 173
Perception of Sensory Imagery • 176
Recognition and Employment of
    Idioms and Figurative Language • 179
Figurative Expressions • 180
Similes and Metaphors • 181
Perception of Mood • 185
Time Period • 186

8. Teaching Critical Comprehension Skills 191

Ability to Make Judgments • 194
Recognition of Fables • 195
Recognition of Satire • 196
Recognition of Myths • 197
Recognition of Irony • 198
Recognition of Fanciful Language • 199
Recognition of Fantasy and Reality • 201
Fact or Opinion—Lesson 1 • 202

Fact or Opinion—Lesson 2 • 204
Identification of Persuasive Techniques • 205
Recognizing Author's Purpose • 208
Altered Syntax • 210
Symbols • 211
Symbolism • 212

9. Modern Approach to Study Skills **215**

Table of Contents • 217
Using the Index • 220
Summarizing • 221
Outlining • 223
Skimming • 224
Scanning • 225
Using the Glossary • 227
Interpreting Graphic Materials • 230
Reading Maps • 234

Index **237**

Teacher's Galaxy of
Reading Improvement Activities —
with model lesson plans

1
Developing the Prereading Skills Requisites

Reading readiness skills are acknowledged as necessary prerequisites to learning word recognition and comprehension skills. Development of criterion-referenced tests has provided evidence that these skills not only are discrete but are also teachable. Therefore, the introduction of students to these prereading skills is necessary before formal reading instruction begins. Without prereading skill knowledge, students will not profit from ordinary reading instruction. But you have the lessons in this chapter to assist you in developing these requisites.

Even though preschool and first grade teachers will be the ones primarily interested in these reading readiness skill lessons, every teacher who has students with severe reading difficulties will find these activities prescriptions for beginning the recovery of these disabled readers. Make use of the lessons on a need-to-learn-basis. If a fifth grader needs auditory discrimination training, provide it; auditory discrimination is a necessary reading readiness skill for a student to have before he can profit from phonics instruction. If the student does not recognize the alphabet, he is not going to learn decoding skills, so teaching the alphabet must precede phonic skill development.

Right away it should be clear to you that there is no such thing as a first grade, a third grade or a seventh grade reading skill. There are only reading skills themselves—which have no way of knowing about administrative designations such as grade levels. The notion that a perfect hierarchical arrangement of reading skills exists is erroneous. Some reading skills provide others as mentioned above, but each teacher, regardless of grade, must be capable of teaching all reading skills because students at all grade levels will have a full range of skill needs. Thus, every teacher of reading will make some use of this chapter.

AUDITORY DISCRIMINATION

Objective: The student will be able to receive and differentiate between auditory stimuli.

Activity suggestions:

1. Make a series of sounds behind a student's back and ask for it to be duplicated:

   Clap three times; stamp foot twice

2. As you read or tell a story, omit a word. Let students supply the word.
3. Say two words behind a student's back. He tells if you say the same word twice or two different words:

   pig—dig
   sit—sit

4. Have students listen to a repeated noise (a clock ticking or a pencil tapping) and raise their hands when the noise stops.
5. Student bounces a ball the same number of times you clap your hands.
6. Say a word that depicts sound, such as "splash," "plop," "crash." Students name things that make that sound.
7. Tape students' voices. Students identify voices.
8. Prepare on cards or on board a series of two-line rhymes to read

and show students. Omit the last word and have students supply rhyming word.

> Look at me,
> High in the _____ (tree).

9. Make several Bingo cards with letters in the squares. Call out several words and ask students to identify the initial sound relationship. Students place marker on the letter:

	words:	kite	jug
_____		milk	pie
<u>b k j</u>		sun	house
		door	butter
<u>f t d</u>		fence	apple
		iron	wish
<u>p w m</u>		tent	gate

(Can also be used for final or middle sounds.)

10. Have students draw a picture of something ending with a stated letter:

—t, —r, 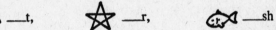—sh

11. Say two words. Have students tell if the words do or do not begin the same:

> boy—bug

AUDITORY MEMORY

Objective: The student will retain and recall information heard.

Activity suggestions:

1. Ask students to make different sounds, such as a dog barking, a motor starting, and so on.
2. Have students act out stories they have heard.
3. Teach students new songs.
4. Ask students what they did last night, last week, last vacation.

5. Have students listen to a short story, then draw a sequence of pictures to tell the story. Have story retold from pictures.
6. Have students name everything they can think of that is red, that you would eat for breakfast, that you would put in the living room, that is hard, and so on.
7. Tape record sounds and have students name them.
8. Say words, letters or numbers in a sequence and have the students repeat them. Then repeat the sequence, omitting one. Have students recall the one omitted. Start with two items and gradually increase the number.
9. Have one student name an object. The next student must name that object and add one of his own, and so on. The game must begin again when a student misses.
10. Have a collection of small objects. Blindfold a student. Give him an object he must identify by feeling only.
11. Read nonsense sentences. Have students correct the sentences:

> Joe put his socks on his hands.
> The bus stopped when the light turned green.
> Mother swept the floor with a mop.
> The dog fell off the ground.

12. Show students an index card or poster board on which pictures have been pasted. Students choose appropriate picture to answer question:

Which one would you wear? (shirt)

Which one spins? (top)

Which one grows? (fish, tree)

Which one is used in a game? (mitt)

Which one can you eat? (fish, cone)

13. Student describes how to do something like sharpen a pencil. Students guess the action from the description.
14. Have two pictures on a card. The students are to identify the appropriate picture:

> The bird is on a house.
> The bird is on a mouse.

15. Say words. Students determine which word does not belong and why:

> bus, truck, apple, car
> Thursday, Christmas, Wednesday, Friday
> A, B, C, 10

VISUAL DISCRIMINATION

Objective: The student will be able to see the difference and similarity in objects.

Activity suggestions:

1. Select two students. Ask another student to tell how they are alike and different.
2. Using blocks, build two simple structures. Have students tell how the structures are alike and different:

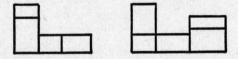

3. Have two pictures of the same object, such as two cats, two tables, etc. Have students tell how they are alike and how they are different.
4. Have two columns of letters, numbers, or words students are to match:

```
a z     4 9
t b     9 4
b t     6 2
z a     2 6
```

5. Have students match unfinished letter, number, or word with finished one:

$$\text{core} = \text{come}$$
$$\text{E} = 8$$
$$\text{7} = Z$$

6. Match words on left with partially completed words on the right:

```
house         __u__p
time       h__ __ __e
jump        __i__e
```

7. Write sentences omitting all vowels. Have students read the sentences:

> Th__ c__t r__n __p th__ tr__ __.
> (The cat ran up the tree.)

8. Using any comic strip, put pictures in a series, adding one that does not belong. Have students choose the one that does not belong in a series.

9. Have students identify all objects in the room that are round, square, red, brown, yellow, etc. (This can be done for lining-up purposes. "Line up at the door if you are wearing green," etc.)

VISUAL MEMORY

Objective: The student will be able to recall a visual image.

Activity suggestions:

1. Have a collection of objects for students to see. Have the students turn their backs while you remove one of the objects. Students turn back to object and decide which object is missing.
2. Have student close his eyes and describe what he or another student is wearing.
3. Play dominoes.
4. Have several objects on a table. The first student touches and names one of the objects. The next player must touch and name the objects touched by the first player, then touch and name another object, and so on. The game ends when a student misses. (Place objects not in a line, but in random order.)
5. Arrange cards in a row. Briefly show a duplicate of one of the cards. Have students point to the identical card in the row of cards.
6. Show a card of letters or numbers for five seconds. Withdraw the card, then have students reproduce card exactly.
7. Have a partially completed drawing for students to finish:

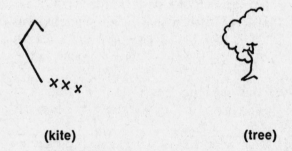

(kite)   (tree)

8. Have students arrange alphabet cards in the correct sequence.
9. Give students a simple geometric design and have students create whatever picture it suggests to them. (This could be done on the chalkboard.)
10. Use toothpicks to create patterns for students to duplicate (see page 28).
11. Have students match capital and lower case letters.

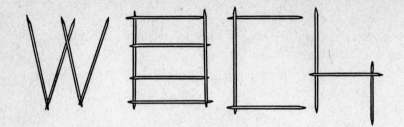

LISTENING

Objective: The student will receive and interpret verbal stimuli.

Activity suggestions:

1. Give simple one-step directions. Gradually increase to two-step and then three-step directions.
2. Ask questions of *who, where, what* after reading a story. Later add *why* questions.
3. Have students tell what they "saw" when you were reading a story.
4. Discuss the characters of a story; how they felt, looked, etc.
5. Have a follow-up discussion of a story you read to students.
6. Tap a pencil on the table or clap your hands several times. The students, with their eyes closed, give the number of sounds they heard.
7. Play games in which students, who are blindfolded, try to identify sounds such as a tapping of a pencil, the crushing of paper, writing on the chalkboard.
8. Go on "listening walks." The students try to discover as many sounds as they can while on the walk. Later make a composite list of sounds heard.
9. Tell or read a story, stopping occasionally to ask questions such as, "Why did Betty want to go with her father?"
10. Set a purpose for listening to a story by asking students to listen for certain things, such as, "Listen to this story to find out what

color dress Mary wanted." For the immature, use basic questions. For more mature students, you could set more abstract listening reasons, such as, "In the story I am going to read something very nice happens to Jimmy. When I have finished reading the story, you tell me why Jimmy deserved all the nice things."

11. Before reading a story, tell the students they are going to arrange some pictures about the story in the sequence in which they relate to the story.
12. Discuss with the students some good listening manners and habits such as looking at the person talking, not talking while someone else talks, and not playing with anything while someone is talking. Evaluation could also be made on how well the students implement their listening habits.
13. Dramatize stories or incidents.
14. Have students listen to three or four numbers, letters, or words, then repeat them in sequence.
15. Read a story, and when finished, make true and false statements about it. If the statement is true, have the student make some motion such as standing, or placing a hand on his head. If the statement is not true, the student does nothing. As a variation, you could make the motion. For true statements the students follow your lead; for false statements, they do nothing.

MOTOR DEVELOPMENT—Body Control

Objective: The student will be able to move the whole body in a coordinated way.

Activity suggestions:

1. Instruct students to:
   Roll from back to stomach.
   Roll from left to right a certain number of times.

    Roll in a somersault.

    Roll backwards in a somersault.

    Roll with a ball between their feet or knees.

2. Have students walk while balancing a book on their heads.
3. Make an obstacle course for students to crawl under a table, over a chair, around a desk.
4. Have students move to the rhythm of music.
5. Point to foot in lead with opposite forefinger when walking.
6. Teach students to jump rope.
7. Have students hop on one foot in place, then on the other foot, then on alternating feet.
8. Use a walking beam.
9. Bending:

    Bend as many parts of your body as you can. Sit, then bend as many parts of your body as you can.

    Bend all the way to the left, to the right. How many parts of your body can you touch with your head?

    Make yourself as tall as you can; as small.

10. Twisting:

    Twist your head without moving anything else.

    Twist your arms around each other; then twist your legs.

    Twist the top of your body only; then the bottom.

11. Stopping:

    Run and stop when I clap my hands or the music stops.

12. Play games such as:

    Pretend you are lifting a heavy load.

    Pretend you are a flower growing.

    Pretend you are a hurricane.

    Pretend you are carrying a heavy load; a light load.

13. Two students face each other. They take turns following the other's movements as if they were in front of a mirror. Note: The entire class can play by having one person lead and all the others follow his movements.
14. Teach children to jump rope, play hopscotch, skip.

MOTOR DEVELOPMENT—Eye-Hand Coordination

Objective: The student will be able to coordinate vision with the movements of the body.

Activity suggestions:

1. Finger paint.
2. Have students make large scribble drawings on the chalkboard, going over the lines many times without lifting the chalk.
3. Have students draw a large circle, then make each succeeding circle smaller. Reverse, starting with a small circle and going to a large circle.
4. Have students draw two circles at the same time.
5. Draw a straight vertical line on the chalkboard and have students duplicate it. Use both hands.
6. Have students draw two vertical lines simultaneously from the top of the chalkboard down.
7. Have students draw a horizontal line on the chalkboard from left to right.
8. Have students trace, then draw, a circle, a square, a rectangle, a diamond.
9. Give much cutting experience.
10. Have construction toys for students.
11. Have students form a circle. One starts by handing a beanbag to the left or right as quickly as possible. If the receiver drops the beanbag or tosses rather than hands it, he is out of the game.
12. Students form a circle. The leader stands in the center of the circle and tosses the ball in the air while calling a player's name. The player called must run forward and catch the ball before it hits the ground. If he misses he is out of the game.
13. Play dodgeball and kickball.
14. Each student has a ball and a partner. The students bounce the balls to their partners. The partner must catch the ball.

ORAL LANGUAGE DEVELOPMENT

Objective: The students will develop fluency and clarity in speaking.

Activity suggestions:

1. Provide many opportunities to:
   Tell about personal experiences.
   Talk about family and pets.
   Tell and retell stories.
   Use puppets.
   Discuss story, film, field trip, etc.
   Describe a picture or situation.
2. Show students pictures and have them name them.
3. Have students name everything they can in the room in a given period of time.
4. Show a picture and say four words of which three relate to the picture. Have students decide which word does not go with the picture and tell why.
5. Have students finish stories started by you or another student.
6. Show pictures of common work objects. Have students tell what they are used for: iron, broom, stove, etc. Also have students tell about different occupations: janitor, mechanic, secretary, etc.
7. Have students give words to describe animals, people, weather, school, library, buildings.
8. Have students answer questions such as:
   How would you tell someone about your new dress/suit?
   How would you get home if you were lost?
   What would happen if you spilled paint?
   What would you need to bake a cake?
   Why would you need to know your telephone number or address?
9. Name various types of transportation and have students describe how each is used:

ambulance	racing car	bicycle
canoe	school bus	police car
tow truck	helicopter	jet plane
garbage truck	station wagon	train

10. Make up word analogies such as: (have students help)

    Bus is to bus stop as train is to depot.

11. Read a sentence several times, emphasizing a different word each time. Students interpret meaning.

    This is my book.   This is *my* book.
    This *is* my book.   This is my *book*?

12. Students come up with original ideas for describing terms:

    Happiness is _____.
    Sadness is _____.

13. Have students complete sentences such as:

    If I were president, _____.
    If I were a grandmother, _____.
    If I were a bus driver, _____.
    If I were Santa Claus, _____.
    If I were a giant, _____.

    and

    How would you feel if:
        you were a flower and someone picked you?
        you were a gingerbread man and the wolf was going
            to eat you?
        you were a book and someone threw you down?

14. Display several pictures. Make a statement about one of the pictures. (See top of following page.) The student identifies the picture for which the statement was made.

Going swimming is fun. (1)
We will have vegetables. (2)
A ride in the country is fun. (3)

You could also ask students to tell in their own words what happened before or after the picture.

15. Ask students to describe the sound associated with certain words.

growl	splat	ring
crash	whooo	buzz
boom	sh	ding-a-ling
squish	ho ho ho	roar

16. Show children a picture. Ask them to name everything they see in the picture. Then with the same picture ask them to tell you something about the picture.

LEFT-TO-RIGHT ORIENTATION

Objective: The student will become acquainted with the direction of left-to-right.

Activity suggestions:

1. Put an X on the left side and an O on the right side of the chalkboard or a piece of paper. Have the students draw a line to connect the X and the O.
2. Write each student's name on a large piece of paper. The student traces over each letter with a crayon. Say each letter as the student traces it.
3. Use the record "Hokey Pokey."
4. Mark papers with a colored symbol for the starting point.
5. Discuss with the students the process of left-to-right and top-to-bottom.
6. Have students draw lines on the chalkboard and trace lines with grease pencils.

7. When you read to students, run your finger under the lines from left-to-right.
8. Set up a display of pocket charts. Using cards bearing letters of the alphabet, distribute the cards randomly to the students. The student holding *A* goes first and puts his card in the first (top left) pocket. The child holding *B* is next and places his card next to the *A*. Continue until all cards are used.
9. Select some things for children to match, placing the ones to be matched on the left.

$$
\begin{array}{ll}
A & 1 \\
L & a \\
T & m \\
M & t
\end{array}
$$

SEQUENCE—PICTURES

Objective: The student will be able to arrange pictures of a series in logical order.

Materials: —two series of three or four pictures for a story
—a series of different pictures for each child (not a story)

Procedure:

1. Read a selection to the students.
2. Ask students to tell you about the story, explaining that they should tell what happened first, next, last. As they tell the story, place the accompanying picture on the chalk ledge when mentioned by the student.
3. Ask if the students agree with the sequence. If yes, go on to step 4. If no, discuss and rearrange in the correct sequence.
4. Repeat steps 1-3 using a different story and set of pictures.
5. Give each student a series of pictures to be put in order as to what would happen first, next, last.

6. Then have each student tell his story according to the sequence he chose.

Extended Activities:

1. Have a student pantomine a task such as getting dressed, planting a garden, or opening a package. Other students are to guess what he is doing.
2. Show a filmstrip without sound, then have students tell a story from the pictures.

SEQUENTIAL ORDER OF EVENTS

Objective: The students will place, in the order of action, sentences from a story read aloud.

Materials: ditto of eight to ten sentences from a story.

Procedure:

1. Read a story to the students.
2. Distribute ditto containing eight to ten sentences in random order, which summarize the story action.
3. Have a student find and read the sentence which comes first in the story.
4. Have all students place a number one (1) at the beginning of that sentence.
5. Continue having students find, read, and number the sentences until all the sentences are numbered in the correct sequential order.

6. Following the numbering, have students read in unison all the sentences, thus forming the complete story.

Extended activities:

1. Cut apart the sentences on the ditto. Paste each sentence, in sequential order, on the bottom part of unlined newsprint. Have students illustrate each page. Put a title on the cover.
2. Print a short paragraph on strips of paper, one sentence per strip. Have students arrange the strips in a logical sequential order.
3. After reading a comic strip aloud to your students, give each one a comic strip that has been cut apart. Have students paste the comic strips in the correct order on a piece of construction paper. Have students then read their comic strips to other children in the group.
4. Use the above procedure with discarded readers.
5. Show a picture. Ask what happened before or after the picture. You can provide choices from which the students can choose.

1. The girl planted a seed. (before)

2. The flower died. (after)

3. The seed sprouted roots. (before)

4. The color of the flower faded. (after)

ALPHABET KNOWLEDGE

Objective: Students will identify upper and lower case letters.

Procedure:

1. Talk about people and objects having names.
2. Talk about letters having names; explain that learning their names helps to remember what they look like.
3. Write the capital letter you wish to teach on the chalkboard. Talk about the way the letter is formed as you write.
4. Say the name of the letter. Have pupils repeat the name.
5. Have pupils write the letter in the air, then on their desk, with their forefingers. They should call the name of the letter each time they write it.
6. Tell pupils that there are two ways to write the letter.
7. Write the small letter on the chalkboard. Talk about how the letter is formed while writing it. Say the name of the letter. Have students repeat the name.
8. Repeat step 5, using lower case letter.
9. Point to each letter, calling each by its name and having pupils repeat the name.
10. Discuss the likeness and differences of the upper and lower case letters.

Extended activities:

1. Write a line of letters, including several of the letters emphasized. Point to each letter. Students say only the name of the letter studied when it is pointed to.
2. After several letters have been introduced, write only a portion of the letters and have students complete it.

3. Eraser Game: Write letters on chalkboard in random order. Child can erase letter if he says the name.

COPYING WORDS

Objective: The student will be able to copy words correctly or write them from memory.

Materials: paper and pencil

Procedure:

1. Have the student trace over words written by the teacher.
2. After student is successful in tracing, have him write under the word or words.
3. Next have the student copy the word or words onto another piece of paper.
4. When successful with step 3, the student can then copy from the chalkboard or chart.

Brief Review—Prereading Skills

You have reviewed the lessons for teaching reading readiness skills so you realize resources are available to you to meet the prereading skill needs of your students. Should some of your students not learn from your lesson—and this is quite natural—then you should teach other skills and subsequently come back to the necessary lesson and repeat it. Your chances for being successful on the second attempt are excellent. In essence, then, if you do not succeed the first time, try again.

2

Keys to Vocabulary and Comprehension

Building sight vocabularies of words and their meanings is always an interesting teaching experience.Vocabulary development is usually not difficult to accomplish as students are responsive to this type of instruction. Also, if you have taught for a while, you know that when given instruction students can build vocabulary power quickly. Rapid increases in your students' word power is rewarding to them and to you.

This chapter contains lessons for teaching synonyms, homonyms, heteronyms, sight vocabulary and multiple meanings of words, giving you the structure for building your students' sight vocabularies. These generic plans are reusable as often as you like. All you need do is substitute new words for the ones in the modules, and you will have the means of attacking underdeveloped vocabularies with intensive treatment and systematically building powerful reading vocabularies in your students.

SYNONYMS

Objective: The student will be able to identify words that have similar meanings.

Materials:　—10 pieces 1½" x 3" red construction paper
　　　　　　　—10 pieces 1½" x 3" pink construction paper
　　　　　　　—felt tip pen
　　　　　　　—masking tape
　　　　　　　—envelope or small box
　　　　　　　—vocabulary words (see boxed list of words); cut
　　　　　　　words apart for distribution to students

Procedure:

1. Tell the children: "There is often more than one way to say something. For example, I could tell your mother that you are very intelligent in Language Arts. 'Smart' and 'intelligent' mean almost the same thing. Many words have similar meanings. Words with similar meanings are called 'synonyms'." Write "smart" and "intelligent" on the chalkboard and label them SYNONYMS.

> **SYNONYMS**
>
> **smart　intelligent**

2. Distribute the vocabulary words to the students. "I have given each of your a word that should be familiar to you. Look at your word and say it to yourself. If you have difficulty, raise your hand, and we will help you. For each word there is a synonym. You have a word and someone else in the group has the synonym for your word. Who can tell us again what a synonym is?"

Activity—Synonym Match:

1. Put two strips of masking tape long enough to hold ten words under SYNONYM on the chalkboard. Turn under a tab to tape to the chalkboard and leave the sticky side out.

small	angry
woods	presents
began	happy
nearly	ended
large	hurry
started	big
glad	almost
forest	gifts
little	stopped
mad	rush

SYNONYMS

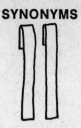

2. Announce: "We are going to play SYNONYM MATCH. Each of you will have a turn to pronounce your word and stick it on the masking tape. If there is already a word on the masking tape that is similar in meaning to your word, put your word on the other tape directly opposite it for a SYNONYM MATCH."

SYNONYMS

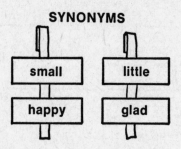

3. When all of the synonyms have been matched, have the group pronounce the word parts. Discuss each pair and have the children create sentences using each of the words in the pairs.

Extending the Activity—Make a Synonym Match Game

1. Now that the synonyms are separated on the strips of masking tape, turn the activity into a SYNONYM MATCH GAME. Choose four children to make the game.

> word cards—2 students
> decorated game container—1 student
> directions—1 student

If you prefer, each child can make a game for individual use.

2. Using the felt tip pen, put each word on a 1½" x 3" piece of construction paper. Use the red construction paper for one masking tape strip and the pink construction paper for the other. The game can be made self-checking by numbering the matching synonyms on the back of the cards.

smart		intelligent		I		I

3. Put the game parts in an envelope or small box.
4. These directions should be included with the game.

    a. Separate the red card from the pink cards.
    b. Take one pile and look at the first word.
    c. Take the other pile and find a word that is a synonym for the first word.
    d. After all the words have been matched, turn the cards over and check to see if you are correct.
    e. Have someone play SYNONYM MATCH with you. Test each other.

5. Additional synonym pairs:

small—little	angry—mad
difficult—hard	stopped—ended
big—large	started—began
grinned—smiled	pouch—bag
level—flat	penny—cent
right—correct	journey—trip
lady—woman	faraway—distant
yell—shout	path—trail
quickly—fast	strange—odd
happy—glad	almost—nearly
forest—woods	gifts—presents
Grandmother—Grandma	rush—hurry
weep—cry	leader—chief
tired—weary	answer—reply
rock—stone	close—near
beautiful—pretty	talk—speak

starved—hungry   afraid—scared
shore—beach   car—automobile

ANTONYMS—Lesson 1

Objective: The student will be able to write antonyms of given words in isolation and in a story.

Materials: student worksheet (see facing page) and pencil

Procedure:

1. Read paragraph about dinosaurs to the class (worksheet, Part A).
2. For discussion and motivation ask students orally: "Describe how it would feel to be a dinosaur. Is that the opposite of how you feel right now?"
3. Write the word *antonym* on the chalkboard. Ask: "What is an antonym? What does opposite mean? Can you think of any words that have antonyms?" Write on chalkboard the student examples of antonyms.
4. Have students read again the paragraph about dinosaurs. This time ask students to notice words in the paragraph that are underlined. Then have students list these words and their antonyms on worksheet (Part B).
5. Have volunteers read their word pairs to the class. Ask for and discuss alternative antonyms.
6. As a supplementary exercise, have students write an antonym for each work on Part C of worksheet.

Extended activity:

Have each pupil draw a dinosaur and then, below his or her drawing, write words that describe it. Have everyone draw an "antonym animal," with features opposite to those listed for the dinosuar. Compare drawings.

ANTONYM WORKSHEET

Part A. READ STORY.

The diplodocus was a dinosaur that lived in <u>ancient</u> times. These were <u>real</u> creatures whose bodies might grow as <u>long</u> as ninety feet or more. But they were quite <u>dangerous</u> to be around, unless you were a <u>plant</u>. The word "dinosuar" means <u>terrible</u> lizard. They were <u>clumsy</u> animals who stayed in the water most of the time because they were too <u>heavy</u> to walk <u>well</u> on land. They had long necks and <u>small</u> heads with nostril <u>openings</u> on top.

Part B. LIST UNDERLINED WORDS FROM STORY AND WRITE ANTONYMS FOR THE WORDS.

1. _____,_____   7. _____,_____
2. _____,_____   8. _____,_____
3. _____,_____   9. _____,_____
4. _____,_____   10. _____,_____
5. _____,_____   11. _____,_____
6. _____,_____   12. _____,_____

Part C. WRITE ANTONYMS FOR THE WORDS LISTED BELOW.

1. often_____   6. immense_____
2. hero_____   7. shiny_____
3. appear_____   8. praise_____
4. prompt_____   9. swift_____
5. confirm_____   10. thoughtful_____

ANTONYMS—Lesson 2

Objective: Students will demonstrate their understanding that antonyms are word opposites.

Materials: flash cards of antonyms

Procedure:

1. Explain that you are going to hold up a card and the students must do what the card says. Use action words such as stop, go; sit, stand; play, work. Discuss the action involved with each word, leading to the understanding that the words mean the opposite of each other.
2. Place word cards on the chalkboard and pass out the word cards of an antonym to the students. Have students place their word cards over the antonym on the chalkboard, saying "＿＿＿ is the opposite of ＿＿＿."
3. Finally, say a word and ask a student to say a word that is opposite to it.

Extended activity:

Construct a wheel out of tagboard. On the wheel put an arrow that will spin around. Divide the wheel into sections and write a word in each section. Divide students into two teams. One player spins the arrow and a member of each team writes on the board an antonym for the word the arrow landed on. The first to write an antonym gets a point.

HOMONYMS

Objective: Students will identify homonym pairs.

Materials: worksheet; one pencil per student

Procedure:

1. Discuss orally with students what homonyms are. (Homonyms are words that sound the same, but have different spellings and different meanings.)
2. Give several examples of homonyms to the students:

> Did you *read* the book? The boat was made of *reed*.
> My *dear* mother gave me a present. The *deer* ran away.
> I have on a *pair* of socks. I ate a *pear* for dinner.

WORKSHEET
FIND THE HOMONYMS

FIND: The missing half of the homonym pairs listed below:

1. see	6. here	11. bear	16. knot
2. him	7. ate	12. cent	17. pair
3. road	8. brake	13. dear	18. meat
4. write	9. whole	14. for	19. seam
5. son	10. hare	15. knew	20. tail

```
h  y  m  n  l  j  u  n  e  i  r  n  g  o  n  t
a  n  o  i  f  l  i  v  n  e  o  t  i  l  n  g
b  h  w  e  g  i  e  u  s  m  d  h  p  h  a  s
e  t  n  h  t  e  s  e  a  l  e  e  t  e  w  f
r  m  u  r  o  d  o  e  m  k  r  s  a  t  a  o
e  i  s  a  m  a  i  l  i  r  u  b  h  a  i  r
t  e  g  e  i  g  h  t  s  t  b  l  o  m  e  d
t  h  t  h  e  x  m  e  r  l  i  r  l  y  a  n
l  e  m  o  t  e  l  e  h  e  w  s  e  e  m  i
n  o  t  d  i  j  r  m  o  n  l  f  l  a  i  w
e  l  w  e  n  a  i  l  d  s  s  o  b  e  k  m
w  e  l  i  b  l  w  i  l  c  i  u  i  t  y  i
w  i  l  v  i  n  e  m  d  e  e  r  t  h  e  t
h  a  v  e  r  e  r  a  b  n  n  d  n  y  e  n
t  a  e  e  a  s  t  w  o  t  h  i  h  i  e  l
l  l  o  t  a  l  e  t  c  i  l  n  a  r  n  m
```

3. Hand out dittos of the worksheet on page 51 to the students.
4. Ask the students to find the hidden homonyms. Tell the students to use the list at the top of the ditto to help them find the correct homonym.
5. Tell the students the homonyms can be located horizontally, vertically, diagonally or backwards.
6. Allow students 30 to 40 minutes.

Extended activities:

1. Have students use the homonym pairs in sentences.
2. Have a contest to see which student can come up with the most homonym pairs. Give a prize to the winner and the runner-up.
3. Make a mobile from homonym pairs and display it in the room.

HETERONYMS

Objective: Students will be able to distinguish differences in pronunciation of heteronyms.

Materials: none

Procedure:

1. Write the following two sentences on the board:

    I read the paper yesterday morning.
    What book do you have to read for class?

2. Ask a student to read each sentence.
3. Circle the word "read" in each sentence.
4. Ask if anyone knows why the same word was pronounced differently in each sentence.
5. Following discussion, explain to students that two words that are spelled alike but sound different are called heteronyms.
6. Write the word "heteronym" on the board and ask students to think of other examples of such words. Write the words on the board as students give them.

7. Ask students to make a sentence with each heteronym, write the sentence on the board, then read the sentences back to students, emphasizing heteronyms.

SIGHT VOCABULARY

Objective: After instruction in techniques of word recognition, students will identify selected words.

Procedure:
1. Introduce the word by showing the flashcard while saying the word.
2. Discuss the meaning of word, when applicable.
3. Use the word in a sentence.
4. Have pupils make up sentences.
5. Have students copy the word on the chalkboard while saying the word.
7. Have students write the word from memory.
8. Repeat steps 1-7 for all words used.
9. (For lesson using more than one word.) Give sentences like those in the sample. Have students hold up flashcards when the vocabulary word completes the sentence.

> *Example:* run
> 1. Mary can _____ faster than Bill.
> 2. I can _____ my bike.

10. (For lessons using more than one word.) Write the words on the chalkboard. Say a sentence omitting one of the words, or ask questions about the words. Have the word identified.

> *Example:* was   run   get
> 1. Which word begins the same as *window*?
> 2. Which word rhymes with *bet*?
> 3. Which word is something you can do?
> 4. I must _____ my coat.
> 5. Bill can _____ fast.
> 6. The dog _____ chasing the cat.

MULTIPLE MEANINGS

Objective: Given selected words, students will demonstrate understanding of meanings.

Materials: —chalkboard
—dictionaries
—paper
—pencils

Procedure:

1. Write the following sentences on the chalkboard:

   The farmer raised wheat.
   He raised a question about math.
   They had raised three children.
   The grocer raised the price of coffee.

   He will iron the shirt.
   I take vitamins with iron.
   The tools were made of iron and steel.

2. Have each of the sentences in the first group read aloud and discuss the underlined word in each one. Ask if the word *raised* means the same thing in each sentence. As each meaning is discovered, write it beside the sentence.
3. Call attention to the second group of sentences and follow the same procedure with each one.
4. Point out that many words have more than one meaning. Write the following words on the chalkboard and have the children give the different meanings for each and use each in a sentence:

class	pen
tire	bark
seat	tape

Extended activities:

1. Show the children how a dictionary can be helpful in identifying

multiple word meanings. Help them look up such words as the following:

test	blocks
meet	mix
fool	water
lying	limp

2. Have the children write or verbalize sentences showing multiple meanings of words they have looked up.

Brief Review–Vocabulary

As you have seen, the vocabulary model lessons in this chapter will enable you to teach your students word knowledge in a variety of ways. Each lesson plan model is usable again and again every time you plan to teach additional vocabulary to your students. As a suggestion, we urge you to make a conscious effort periodically, say once every week or two, to teach word knowledge. By systematizing your word building program, you will not run the risk of neglecting the development of these building blocks of reading power, but you will make use of a cumulative strategy which will move your readers assuredly to higher reading levels.

3

Context Clues for Discovering New Words

Mature readers use context clues to decode unknown words ninety-five per cent of the time. High usage of this word recognition skill is evidence of its value to readers. Needless to say, context clue development needs to be taught effectively, and to this end, several lessons are provided.

Because this reading skill is so important we have developed core Lesson 15 into three parts—A, B, and C. Begin your instruction by using part A, and continue through the other parts, B and C, as time allows. You may need from seven to ten days or longer in teaching this material since each lesson contains extended activities for reinforcing the skill development. After you have taught all three parts of Lesson 15, develop with your students the specialized context clue lessons (16–19), which relate to understanding the use of synonyms, antonyms and homographs in unlocking unknown words. Attention given to this reading skill using these lessons will pay dividends as your students exercise this skill in attacking unknown words.

USING CONTEXT CLUES—Lesson 1

Objectives: (1) The student will be able to determine the meaning of unknown and unfamiliar words by analyzing the context of the sentence.

(2) The student will be able to construct sentences that demonstrate context clues to determine meaning of a given vocabulary word.

Materials: use of chalkboard; dittoed handout for practice

Procedure:

1. Write the following sentences on the board and ask students to provide words to fill the blanks.

   "A deep-toned bell _____ over the hills."

   (POSSIBLE RESPONSES: rang, tolled, sounded)

   "The huge green frog _____ over the rocks."

   (POSSIBLE RESPONSES: leaped, hopped, jumped)

2. Explain to the students that other words in a sentence can give clues to the meanings of words that are unfamiliar. Sometimes they're obvious, as in the examples above. Sometimes the clues are only hints at the meaning of the word. Emphasize that use of context clues can be for them an important tool in decoding unknown vocabulary words.

3. Write on the board two examples of relatively unfamiliar words in sentences containing context clues.

   "The body was swept into the deep, <u>fathomless</u>, ocean bed and was never found."

   (POSSIBLE RESPONSES: bottomless, very deep, unknown depths)

   "The man studied <u>meteorology</u> in college, and went on to become a weatherman for station WKGB in Los Angeles."

   (POSSIBLE RESPONSES: weather study)

   Following each example, discuss what words or groups of words gave clues to the meaning of the unknown word.

4. If students still seem unsure of context usage, put a few more examples on the board.

5. Give students a series of sentences with an unfamiliar word un-

derlined in each. Ask gives a clue to the word's meaning. Then ask them to write what they think the unknown word means.

Extended activities:

1. Give students a short list of unknown words. Have them look up the meanings in the dictionary; then, for each word, construct a sentence that contains a clue to its meaning.
2. For variety, give each student a word which he is to look up and for which he then writes a sentence containing a context clue. Students exchange papers and try to figure out the meaning of the unknown word.
3. Have students look in magazines for sentences which help define words by using context clues. They may either copy them from the magazine or clip them for display and class discussion under the opaque projector.
4. Take time to identify context clue usage in paragraphs of material encountered in the classroom.
5. Have students keep a list of context clue sentences as they read as a practice in becoming more aware of this valuable reading tool.

USING CONTEXT CLUES—Lesson 2

Objective: Using the context of a sentence, a student will identify an unknown word.

Materials: none

Procedure:

1. Write a sentence containing a made-up word.

   The children were breathing fast because they <u>ruttled</u> up the hill.

2. Ask if anyone knows the meaning of <u>ruttled</u>.

3. Read the sentence to the children.
4. Ask what they think <u>ruttled</u> means when they think about the whole sentence.
5. Write all their suggestions on the chalkboard. Discuss each.
6. Repeat steps 1 to 5, using other sentences containing made-up words.
7. Remind students that reading the entire sentence helps them identify and understand unknown words.

Extended activity:

Have sentences prepared containing made-up words. Under the sentences have a choice of three possible answers. Students are to select the answer that makes sense in the sentence. Be sure the sentences are on the students' reading level:

> The <u>fant</u> licked the milk from the dish.
> a. tree   b. <u>kitten</u>   c. boy

USING CONTEXT CLUES—Lesson 3

Objective: The student will supply missing words through understanding of the context of a sentence.

Materials: flash cards of words to be used in sentences

Procedure:

1. Write sentences containing unknown words:

> The dog <u>chased</u> the cat.
> My mother <u>scolded</u> me for playing too long.
> The monkey chattered <u>happily</u> while swinging from tree to tree.

2. Ask students to read first sentence, skipping unknown words.
3. Have students supply words they think would make sense in the sentence by thinking, "What does a dog usually do to a cat?"
4. Repeat steps 2 and 3 with each sentence.

5. Erase the underlined words from the sentences. Pass out flash cards containing the words erased.
6. Read each sentence aloud. As you get to the blank, the child holding the card that "makes sense in the sentence" stands up while showing the card.

Extended activities:

1. Have prepared sentences in which a word is omitted. Let students supply missing words of their choice that make sense in the sentence.
2. Have prepared sentences with a word omitted and several choices. Student chooses word:

> The beach was _____ with people.
> (a) overcrowded   (b) washable   (c) deserted

HOMOPHONES IN CONTEXT

Objective: The student will demonstrate ability to use context clues in choosing the appropriate homophone.

Materials: none

Procedure:

1. On the chalkboard, write a word that has more than one meaning, such as *fair*. Have students give as many meanings as they can for the word.
2. Use the word in a sentence and ask what the meaning of the word is in the sentence:

> It's not fair!
> We can go to the fair.

3. Continue the same procedure using other words, such as *can*, *school*, etc.
4. Put a list of words on the chalkboard and have students supply their homophones. Talk about the meanings of each:

buy	by
weigh	way
heal	heel
piece	peace

5. Lead students to understand that the sentence in which the word is used is the determiner of which word to use:

   I would like a _____ of cake.   (piece)
   I would like some _____ and quiet.   (peace)

Extended activities:

1. Have students choose correct meaning:

piece	heaviness
peace	a part
wait	freedom from war
weight	to delay

2. Finish sentences by choosing correct word:

   The bicycle (pedal, peddle) was broken.
   An animal is a (deer, dear).

SELECTING CORRECT SYNONYMS

Objective: Students will be able to write synonyms for given words and substitute them for selected words in a story.

Materials: student worksheet and pencil

Procedure:

1. Read story about Tyrannosaurus Rex to the class (Part A—worksheet).
2. For discussion ask: "What words would you use to describe a dinosaur? Do any of these words mean the same thing? Are they synonyms?"
3. Write the word *synonym* on the chalkboard. Ask: "What is a synonym? Why do you suppose there are many words that mean

the same thing? How do you find out the exact meaning of a word? How are the meanings of words determined? Can the meanings of words change? How?"

WORKSHEET SELECTING CORRECT SYNONYMS

PART A: READ STORY

As an eater of plants, diplodocus was no threat to other animals, but other dinosaurs stalked smaller animals and consumed their meat. These flesh-eaters had long tails and galloped around on two legs. The most terrible of these monsters was fifty feet long and twenty-five feet high. Its head was large and filled with sharp teeth. It was called "Tyrannosaurus Rex," which means king of the lizards.

An unusual thing about this giant is that its arms were too short to reach its mouth.

Scientists can only speculate why the dinosaur eventually became extinct.

Part B: LIST UNDERLINED WORDS FROM THE STORY AND WRITE SYNONYMS FOR THE WORDS.

1. _____,_____   7. _____,_____
2. _____,_____   8. _____,_____
3. _____,_____   9. _____,_____
4. _____,_____   10. _____,_____
5. _____,_____   11. _____,_____
6. _____,_____

Part C: WRITE SYNONYMS FOR THE WORDS BELOW.

1. create _____   6. popular _____
2. jump _____   7. disease _____
3. conclude _____   8. genuine _____
4. laugh _____   9. endure _____
5. labor _____   10. male _____

4. Have students read the story, asking them to notice underlined words in the paragraph. These are words to be replaced with a synonym. Remind the students that synonyms are words that have the same meaning.
5. Have students list the underlined words from story and give a synonym for each (Part B—worksheet).
6. Have volunteers read the synonyms they wrote. Ask for alternative synonyms.
7. As a supplementary exercise, have students write a synonym for each word given on Part C of the worksheet.

Extended activity:

Have a volunteer stand with his back to the board. Write a word on the board. Have the class give synonyms for that word until the volunteer guesses it.

RECOGNIZING ANTONYMS IN CONTEXT

Objective: The students will be able to recognize and choose antonyms.

Materials: supplementary materials for independent work and group activity

Procedure:

1. Write sentences on the chalkboard, underlining the word to be replaced by its opposite:

> The boy was very big.
> The stairs will take us up.
> The man in the circus is very strong.

Write the opposites to be used in a list on the chalkboard:

    down
    weak
    little

2. Have the students choose the correct opposite trom the list to go into the sentences.
3. Discuss opposites with the students; ask for examples of opposites.
4. Write sentences on the chalkboard, underlining the word to be replaced by its opposite. Omit listing of words this time:

> The <u>boy</u> went to the fair.
> The gas tank was <u>full</u>.
> The weather has been very <u>hot</u> lately.

5. Have the students supply the opposites for each sentence.

Extended activities:

1. Concentration game with opposites. Tape 36 cards made of construction paper on the chalkboard. The cards will be numbered on the front and have a word written on the back. There will be 18 pairs of opposites. Divide the class into two teams. Each team tries to find the opposites in an alternating pattern. If one team gets a pair, they get another chance, although a different student on that team should take a turn at guessing. Points are awarded for each pair guessed and the score is kept. When a student guesses a pair, the cards are given to him until the end of the game. At the end, it is fun to see who has the most cards.
2. Crossword puzzle ditto on antonyms for independent work. (See page 68.)

Directions—To complete this puzzle, you must use the antonym for the words given.

<u>Across:</u>	<u>Down</u>
1. day	1. always
5. no one	2. boy
6. you	3. these
7. begin	4. live

HOMOGRAPHS IN CONTEXT

Objective: Students will understand that homographs are words that are spelled the same but are pronounced differently and have different meanings.

Materials: none

Procedure:

1. Write two homographs on the chalkboard, including the phonetic marking, i.e.: wĭnd — wīnd
2. Have the words pronounced. Discuss the differences in the pronunciation, and the identical spelling.
3. Write the two following sentences on the board:
   The _____ blew hard.
   We had to _____ the clock every night, or it would stop.
4. Have students decide on the pronunciation of the word "wind" in each of the sentences.

5. Have students suggest other homographs, and write each phonetically on the board as students call them out.
6. Have students make sentences with each set of homographs.

Extended activity:

Read an incomplete sentence and reveal homographs on flash cards. Students select the correct homograph from the cards.

Brief Review—Context Clues

Now that you have taught the lessons in this chapter, you probably realize that your effort to make your students become word detectives is paying off. Making your students independent decoders is naturally a result of context clue development. Even though you may have had some success, we suggest occasional returns to these lessons for review. New words are easily transposed for the originals, or an extended activity might be repeated. Too, any return will pay dividends, so do provide context clue review for your students.

4

Teaching Sound and Symbol Recognition (Phonics)

Recognition of letter-sound relationships is an important word attack skill. In reality, phonics is a term used to describe a multitude of skills, from knowing single letter sound representations to the recognition of multiple letters standing for several sounds or sounding elements. In this chapter you have a wealth of lessons to assist you in helping your students become strong decoders. From teaching initial and ending consonants to blends and digraphs and from teaching short and long vowels through silent and r-controlled vowels, this chapter will enable you to be a proficient teacher of phonics.

Begin teaching the consonant letter sounds first. Not only are they easier to learn because they are not as variable as vowel sounds, but they are also more important and useful to the decoder. Consonants are strong sound units of language, and beginning sound-letter discrimination with consonants is logical. Stressing symbols representing vowel sounds is important, too. Although vowel sounds function as connectors between consonants and are not particularly dominant, their relative sound representation is less stable than consonants, and therefore they are considerably more difficult to teach and learn.

Since there are many lessons in this chapter, you may want to intersperse other skill development lessons from other chapters, or space them out with recreational reading, to keep students from being bored with too much sound-symbol recognition. Eventually, all lessons in this chapter should be taught, as phonics is the heart of word attack development.

INITIAL CONSONANTS (Single)—Auditory

Objective: To provide pupils with instruction in the recognition, discrimination, and reproduction of initial consonant sounds.

Materials: eight to ten pictures, some beginning with the sound being taught and some beginning with other sounds

Procedure:

(Note: Have one model word for each sound you are teaching to be used throughout each lesson. This lesson uses the model word *sat* for developing the initial sound of *s*. The procedure would be the same for any letter.)

1. Say two words beginning with different sounds, but ending alike: *sat—pat*
2. Ask if the words are the same. Discuss what makes them different.
3. Repeat the words and ask if a different sound is heard at the beginning of the words.
4. Discuss the different beginning sounds of *sat—pat*.
5. Say two words with the same initial sound: *sat—sip*.*
6. Ask if *sat* and *sip* begin with the same sound. Have pupils repeat the words.
7. Using other words, ask students to identify the words that begin the same as *sat*. Use words that do and do not:

---

*Emphasize the initial sound as you say the words.

Does *sap* begin the same as *sat*?
Does *man* begin the same as *sat*?

8. Use eight or ten pictures, some beginning with the sound of *s* and some beginning with other sounds. Have pupils identify *s* pictures.

Extended activities:

1. Sound Book. Have pupils find pictures of objects beginning with a certain sound. Paste on a page in book—one sound per page.
2. Say some sentences containing several words beginning with the same sound. Pupils repeat the sentence, identifying the words beginning with the same sound.
3. Use a picture containing several objects beginning with the same sound. Have pupils identify these objects.

INITIAL CONSONANTS (Single)—Visual

Objective: To provide instruction in associating the letter sound to the symbol.

Materials: individual letter cards; picture of object beginning with sound being taught

Procedure:

1. Show a picture card or write a word beginning with the initial sound being taught.
2. Ask pupils to name the letter that stands for the beginning sound of the picture or word.
3. Write the letter on the chalkboard. Have pupils repeat the name of the letter.
4. Using the model picture or word, give three or four examples of other words with the same beginning sound:

Does *seen* begin the same as *sat*?

Write each word used on the chalkboard in a column.

5. After all the words have been written on the chalkboard, have pupils repeat all the words. They may also underline the first letter of each word as they say the word.
6. Distribute the individual letter cards to each pupil. Say a list of words and have pupils hold up the card each time they hear a word beginning with that sound.

Extended activities:

1. Have pupils change the first letter of familiar words to the letter being studied:

   > *mat* to *sat*
   > *pet* to *set*

2. Have pupils find and list all the words beginning with a certain sound from a story they have read, a newspaper, a magazine, etc.

INITIAL CONSONANTS
(Single)—Application

Objective: To provide instruction in combining context and initial sound.

Materials: picture cards representing several initial sounds

Procedure:

1. Display three picture cards at a time, one with the initial sound being taught and two with other sounds.
2. Say a sentence in which a word is omitted. The omitted word should be the displayed picutre with the initial sound being taught. Tell pupils the sound they are looking for:

   > I like to sit in the s____.
   >   (sun)

3. Have pupils tell why they did not choose the remaining pictures.
4. Repeat steps 1, 2 and 3, using different pictures, always including one picture with the initial sound being taught.

Extended activities:

1. Read a short paragraph aloud, omitting the words beginning with a designated sound. Have students supply the words:

> Sue wanted to buy a gift for her s⎯⎯.
> (sister)
> She didn't have enough money. She s⎯⎯ down in the s⎯⎯
> to think.   (sat)   (sun)

2. Play a game in which the responses must begin with the same sound: "I went to the store and bought a s⎯⎯, s⎯⎯, and s⎯⎯." Students can supply the words or teacher can say them and students decide if they are correct.
3. After several sounds have been discussed, omit a word from a sentence, showing the letter the word should begin with. Have pupils supply words:

> I like to spend m⎯⎯.
> (money)
> I gave a bone to my d⎯⎯.
> (dog)

ENDING CONSONANTS

Objective, Students will recognize and sound out ending consonants.

Materials: none

Teaching Procedure:

1. Say a single word and have pupils repeat it:

Say word normally — fig
Say it slowly   — fi- -g

2. Ask pupils what letter represents the last sound in the word *fig*.
3. Say other words ending with /g/, such as *swig, gig,* and *gang*. Ask students if the words end the same as *fig* and to identify the letter representing the final sound. Point out that all words end with *g*.
4. Write a column of words with the same final sound and read the words, pointing to the last letter as you say each word. Slightly emphasize the final sound.
5. Ask pupils in what way these words sound alike, then what letter stands for the last sound. Have students underline the last letter in each word.
6. Write a list of words on the chalkboard and have pupils change the last letter in each word to the letter you are teaching. Pupils pronounce new words:

> but to bug
> ran to rag
> bad to bag
> did to dig

Extended activity:

After several consonant sounds have been taught, play Auditory Bingo. Distribute a Bingo card with letters in each square, making sure cards have letters arranged differently. Call the list of words. Pupils cover the letter on the card representing the final sound of the word called.

B	I	N	G	O
g	d		t	
m	n		u	
f	r		i	

B	I	N	G	O
u	i		g	
m	f		t	
n	r		d	

Call these words: muff   bug   star   sun
                   bat   sock   jam   fall

CONSONANT BLENDS (Visual-Auditory)

Objective: Student will recognize and discriminate consonant blends.

Materials: none

Procedure:

(Note: Make sure pupils know single consonant sound before teaching blends.)

1. Discuss with pupils the fact that in many words there are two or three consonants before the first vowel.
2. Give some example, such as: "What letter can you hear that is combined with *s* to make the beginning sound in *star*?" (Slightly elongate the beginning sound.)
3. Write the word *star* on the chalkboard. Underline the *st*.
4. Ask pupils to listen to other words and listen for the two letters that stand for the beginning sound. Pronounce words in which the blend being taught is used. Write each word on the chalkboard. Slightly emphasize the initial blend.
5. Have pupils identify the first two letters of each word:

    <u>bl</u>ue
    <u>bl</u>ouse
    <u>bl</u>ack

6. Say, "Now listen as I say four words. Listen for the sound at the beginning of each word."
7. Discuss how the words are alike.
8. On the chalkboard, write four words containing the initial blend you are teaching. Call attention to the initial blend.
9. Say three words—two that begin with the same blend, and one

that does not. Have students identify the one that does not begin the same.

10. Say three words—two that begin with the same blend and one that does not. Pupils identify the two that do begin the same.

11. Have pupils say other words beginning with the blend being taught.

CONSONANT BLENDS (Association and Application)

Objective: Student will demonstrate knowledge of consonant blends/sound relationships and application to words.

Materials: none

Procedures:

1. Write some words beginning with the blend you are teaching in a column on the chalkboard. Make sure the blends are directly under each other.

2. Pronounce the words and have pupils underline only the initial blends in each word.

3. Write some sight words on the chalkboard. These should be words in which the consonant blend can be substituted for the initial sound to form new words. Have pupils read new words:

write	change to
sack	black
sue	blue

(Step 3 can be done by the teacher substituting each of the blends for the initial sound and having the pupil give the new word, or by the teacher giving the new word and having the pupils tell the letters to be substituted.)

4. Write some sentences on the chalkboard in which the word con-

taining the blend is partially omitted. Have pupils read the sentence and supply the missing word:

> Mary's dress is bl___.

Extended activities:

1. Rhyming game: I am thinking of a word that begins like *black* and rhymes with sock. (block)
2. Say words. Pupils write the initial blend only when they hear a word that begins with a designated blend. After several have been learned, pupils can write the initial blend for all words said by teacher.

R-BLENDS

Objectives: The students will be able to recognize and write initial r-blends: br, cr, dr, fr, gr, pr, and tr.

Materials: a worksheet having words with the initial r-blends to be completed by the students

Procedure:

1. Write this sentence on the board: "The trapeze artist dropped a pretty green branch with crimson flowers in front of the audience."
2. Ask a student to name the first word that begins with an r-blend and write above it the letters that form the blend.
3. Continue in the same way until the seven initial r-blends have been identified.
4. Begin with the first blend, tr, and have students name other words that begin with that blend.
5. Continue this procedure with the other blends.

Extended Activities:

1. To make sure students distinguish between consonant blends and consonant digraphs, pronounce the following words and tell students to write only those that begin with blends:

chime	greet	drink	cheese
crime	sheet	brink	breeze
bring	then	think	frozen
thing	trend	these	chosen

2. Give students these words and ask them to make as many words as they can by substituting r-blends for the initial consonant or consonant digraph in each word: dim, pain, less, shy, new, lace, chief, sand, dash, jumble.

OTHER CONSONANT BLENDS (sc, sk, sl, sm, sn, sp, st, sw)

Objectives: Students will recognize blend elements and demonstrate ability to use symbol-sound relationship in decoding unknown words.

Materials: chalkboard and dittoed worksheet

Procedure:

1. Write the following blend words on the board:

    scat – skate – slam – small – snake – speed – state – swing

    Say the words, pointing out that your listeners should listen for the sounds of the first two letters.

2. Ask your students to say words containing these blends and list their responses under the key words on the board. For stimulation, you may want to start by asking them to look around the room for objects or pictures. (For a student, being allowed to write a choice on the board is motivating and rewarding.)

3. Ask that everyone say the first word under *scat* together. Select one pupil to come to the board and circle the blend representing the /sc/ sound. Continue until your judgment tells you further activity will be counterproductive.
4. Pass out dittoed worksheet.

WORKSHEET—CONSONANT BLENDS

LOOK AT THE PICTURES. SAY THE WORDS. Find the same beginning sounds in the words below each picture. For example, the first picture is a boy smiling. The SM is underlined in smile, smell, and small because these words have the same beginning sounds.

<u>SM</u>ILE
SKIP
SLAP
<u>SM</u>ELL
<u>SM</u>ALL

SPELL
STAR
STEP
SNAIL
START

SMOKE
SKIRT
SKIP
SNOW
SWELL

SLED
SWING
SWIM
SMALL
SMART

SNAKE
SPOON
SPADE
SHADE
SNAP

SCAR
SMUG
SCOOTER
SCALE
SCOUT

SLED
SCOUT
SKIT
SLATE
SLEEP

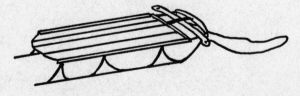

SPIN
SPIDER
SPACE
SKIRT
SPEED

Extended activities:

1. On 3x5 index cards, write the blends you want your students to learn:

2. On separate cards draw pictures that represent words with designated blends. On the back, write the word for the picture:

3. Pass out the picture cards to your students and lay the blend cards across the table.
4. Have your students put their picture cards under the correct blend card. They can turn the cards over to see that they are right.
5. Pass out blank index cards, asking your pupils to draw a picture of a word containing the designated blend you mention.

CONSONANT DIGRAPHS

Objective: Students will form words beginning with the consonant digraphs ch, sh, th, and wh.

Materials:—at least two pictures representing each digraph sound
—dictionaries and spelling books

Procedure:

1. Start lesson by placing four pictures on the board, such as sheep, chair, thimble, and wheel.
2. Discuss with students the sounds the consonant digraphs represent which are the beginning sounds in these words. Have them repeat them several times, noting that two letters represent only one sound.
3. Show more pictures and see if students can correctly place these pictures under the first four. *Examples:* shelf, whale, church, three.
4. Explain that today we are going to study words that begin with these sounds by playing a game called *Password* on the board. Tell students that each time they wish to perform a duty, get a drink, run an errand, they must give a new password with that sound. Each new word is added to the board.
5. Allow students to use any source for assistance—spelling book, dictionaries etc.—to help expand their vocabulary.
6. At the end of the day, allow time to go over the list, and place the words under the correct pictures.

Extended activities:

1. Have students work in groups, placing small pictures under the correct beginning sounds.
2. Explain that these sounds may also be found at the end of a word. Have students do some ditto pages on which they draw a circle around the letters that tell how the word-picture begins or ends.
3. Relay. Divide the class into teams of five or six players for a re-

view. Each team has a different digraph—ch, sh, th, or wh. When the teacher says, "Go," the first member of each team goes to the board and writes a word beginning with his digraph. If a student can't think of a word, he passes. The winning team is the group that has completed the largest number of words during a specified time.

SHORT VOWELS

Objective: Students will recognize short vowel sounds in words.

Materials: several pictures of objects that do and several of objects that do not contain the short vowel sound

Procedure:

1. Write a list of familiar words that contain the short vowel sound you are teaching.
2. Point to the vowel in each word as you pronounce the word.
3. Say, "Sometimes the letter ____ sounds the way it does in these words."
4. Repeat the words, then isolate the sound of the vowel. (Isolate vowel sound only in beginning instruction, and with pupils having difficulty.)

    sat — a   map — a

5. Pronounce other words and have students raise their hands only when they hear the vowel sound you are teaching. Explain that some words will and some will not have the vowel sound.
6. Place pictures along the chalk ledge. Have pupils identify the ones with the vowel sound being taught.
7. Have pupils say some other words they can think of that have the vowel sound of the lesson.

Extended activities:

1. Have pupils find pictures of objects containing vowel sound being emphasized.

2. Have pupils substitute vowel sound being taught and read word:

     p<u>i</u>n to p<u>a</u>n

3. Write words omitting the vowel. Pupils supply vowel and pronounce word:

     h ——— t
     m ——— p

4. Write a sentence omitting the vowel. Pupils supply vowel, then read the sentence:

     Mother h ——— s a new h ——— t.

LONG VOWELS

Objective: Students will recognize long vowel sounds in words.

Materials: pictures of objects that do and objects that do not contain the long vowel sound being taught

Procedure:

1. Write the vowel for the lesson on the chalkboard. Talk about it.
2. Write a column of familiar words containing the long vowel being taught in a column on the chalkboard.
3. Pronounce each word, slightly elongating the vowel sound. Point to the vowel as you say the word.
4. Discuss the vowel sound.
5. Ask pupils to listen for the containing vowel sound you are teaching. Have pupils pronounce the words after you. Do not write the words.
6. Discuss how the vowel said its own name in each word. Give as much practice as needed.
7. Place pictures along the chalk rail. Some pictures should contain the vowel sound of the lesson and some should not. Have pupils select only the pictures with the long vowel sound of the lesson.

8. Have pupils say other words containing the long vowel sound of the lesson.

Extended activities:

1. Have pupils find pictures of objects containing the long vowel sound in magazines.
2. Write a column of words omitting the vowel. Have pupils fill in vowel, then read the word:

> b _____ t (boat)
> s _____ p (soap)

3. Write a sentence omitting the long vowel sound. Pupils supply vowels and read sentence:

> The b _____ t sailed on the s _____.

4. Make large boat. Have pupils supply as many long vowels as possible:

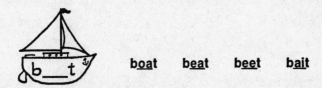

b**oa**t   b**ea**t   b**ee**t   b**ai**t

SHORT AND LONG VOWELS
(Differentiating Between)

Objective: After visual and auditory practice, the pupils will be able to discriminate between long and short vowel sounds in words.

Materials:
—3" x 5" card for each student
—pictures of objects containing both the long and short vowel used
—a picture for other vowel sounds

Procedure:

1. Give each pupil a 3"x5" card. He writes the same vowel on both sides of the card. Have the pupil draw a line over one vowel (ā) and a curved line over the other (ă).
2. Ask pupils to show you the long vowel, then the short vowel. Make sure all pupils know which is which.
3. Pronounce words that have both the long and the short vowel sound. Have pupils hold up their cards, displaying the side of the card that shows the vowel sound heard. Give as much practice as needed.
4. Place picutres of objects containing both vowel sounds and some with other vowel sounds along chalk rail. Ask students to choose pictures of objects with the short vowel sound, with the long vowel sound, and the pictures with neither.

Extended activities:

1. Vowel substitution: Make new words by substituting the vowel sounds:

    hit to hat
    lake to like

2. Have pupils tell what vowel they would substitute in the words at the left at the sentence so the new words will make sense in the sentence:

    (pat) Bill has a _____ mouse.
    (like) We can swim in the _____.

SILENT VOWEL SOUNDS

Objective: Students will be able to recognize that certain words sometimes contain vowels that are not sounded in pronouncing the word.

Materials: none

Procedure:

1. Write the word "lie" on the board.
2. Ask the students if they can hear the "e" sound in this word, or if they just hear the "1" and the "i."
3. Write the word "bake" on the board.
4. Ask students if they can hear the "e" in this word.
5. Explain that there are some words in our language that have vowels in them that are not sounded.
6. Ask students to think of words with silent vowels.
7. Write the words on the board and circle the silent vowel at the students' direction as they call the words out.

R-CONTROLLED VOWELS

Objective: Students will be able to recognize that vowels make sounds that are neither short nor long, when they precede the letter "r" in a word ending in that letter.

Procedure:

1. Write the following words on the board:

> far
> car
> star

2. Ask students what each of these words have in common.
3. Answers may be that they rhyme, they sound alike, they all end in "r," etc.
4. Write the words:

> cat
> tale

on the board under the first three words.
5. Ask students whether the "a" in *far* sounds like the "a" in *cat*.

6. Ask students whether the "a" in *star* sounds like the "a" in *tale*.
7. Continue this activity until you have compared all the words on the board with each other.
8. Emphasize that when words end in "r" and have a vowel before the "r," that vowel will be neither long, as in *tale*, nor short, as in *cat,* but will have a sound all its own, related to the "r" on the end of the word.
9. State that we call this rule of pronounciation the rule of the "r-controlled vowel," because the "r" controls the sound the vowel makes.

Extended activity:

Have students go to the board and construct sentences using one word with a short or long vowel sound, and one word with an r-controlled vowel sound. Give a sample sentence, such as, "My mother told me a short *tale* about a dog that learned to drive a *car*." Point out that *tale* is a word with a long vowel sound, and *car* has a r-controlled vowel sound. Have students read back their sentences aloud and point out the word with the long or short vowel, and then the word with the r-controlled vowel.

VOWEL COMBINATIONS

Objective: Given words with vowel combinations, students will demonstrate ability in recognizing the sounds represented.

Materials: cards prepared as in step 7 for words listed on chalkboard in step 1

Procedure:

1. Write a list of words containing the vowel combination you are teaching. Use one-syllable words. Pronounce the words.
2. Have pupils identify the first and last sound in the first word.
3. Have pupils identify the middle sound of the word.

4. Ask if both letters in the middle can be heard:

   b e̲ a̲ t

5. Ask pupils to name the two letters they see in the middle of the word.
6. Ask what sound these letters make when they are together. (Repeat steps 1-6, using each word in the list.)
7. Have prepared cards for each word listed on chalkboard in the following format:

Pupils pronounce only the part of word that is underlined.

Extended activities:

1. Have a column of words omitting the vowel combinations. Read the words. Have pupils fill in the vowel:

   b (o̲ a̲) t
   s (o̲ a̲) p

2. When several combinations have been studied, use different ones. Teacher reads word, pupils fill in vowel combination:

   b (o̲ y)
   fl (o̲ a̲) t
   c (o̲ w)
   (a̲ w) ful

RHYMING WORDS—Lesson 1

Objective: Student will recognize and reproduce rhyming elements in words.

Materials: none

Procedure:

1. Write two rhyming words on the chalkboard, such as *cat, bat*
2. Say, "One of these words says *cat*. Which one?
3. Ask what the first letter in the word *cat* is.
4. Have pupils identify the letters in *cat* that are the same in *bat*. Underline the letters that are the same in both words.
5. Repeat steps 1-4, using other rhyming words such as *cake, make; can, fan*.
6. Write only one word, such as *man*. Say the word as you write it.
7. Write an *r* under the *m* in *man*.
8. Ask pupils what two letters you would have to write to make the word *ran*. Write them.
9. Continue with step 8, using other words.
10. Lead pupils to understand that words that end with the same sound are called rhyming words. Have pupils identify the rhyming part of all the words used in the lesson.

Extended activities:

1. Say three words in which two rhyme and one does not. Have pupils identify the two that rhyme or the one that does not. Words can be written on the chalkboard as you say them. Pupils can then underline the rhyming part.
2. Read two-line poems, allowing pupils to supply the rhyming word in the second line:

> I was sitting on the rug.
> And I saw a little ———.

> My master was a dog,
> but I was a ———.

> Alice was fat.
> So was the ———.

RHYMING WORDS—Lesson 2

Objective: Students will understand that words can rhyme without ending with the same letters.

Materials: none

Procedure:

1. Put a word on the chalkboard and ask students to name all the words that rhyme with it. List the words.
2. Ask the students to help you make two lists of the words on the board; one containing the words with the same final spelling and the other those that do not have the same spelling:

<u>good</u>	hood stood	should could	
<u>blow</u>	go so no	sew	throw know
<u>high</u>	try my	thigh sigh	

3. Help students discover that words do not have to look alike to rhyme, but must sound alike.

Extended activities:

1. Using flash cards made up of rhyming words, students can team up and make short poems, using rhyming words that have the same or variant spelling endings.
2. Students may test each other's ability to identify rhyming words with the same or variant spelling endings.

BLENDING WORD ELEMENTS—Lesson 1

Objective: Students will be able to blend separate sound elements into a word.

Materials: none

Procedure:

1. Draw three circles on the chalkboard. Put consonants in the first circle, vowels in the second, and consonants in the third.

2. Have a student choose a letter from each circle and write them on the chalkboard:

   sat – met – tan

   Have him say the sound, holding it until the next letter is chosen:

   s-s-s-s-s-a-a-a-a-a-t (sat)

3. Continue until each student has had a turn.
4. You say some sound elements very slowly, having students identify the word:

   say, "m-m-m-m   a-a-a-a   t" (mat)

Extended activity:

Cut small squares from tagboard and print a letter on each. Make several for each letter of the alphabet. Store them in an egg carton. Students can make words by using the letters.

2 letters to a place.

A,B – C,D – and so on.

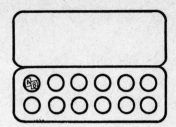

BLENDING WORD ELEMENTS—Lesson 2

Objective: Students will be able to blend separate word parts into words.

Materials: none

Procedure:

1. Write two words on the chalkboard, underlining the part of the words you wish to use:

   <u>br</u>ight
   t<u>akes</u>

2. Have the words identified.
3. Write a sentence omitting the word the underlined parts would make:

   The train was going too fast and had to put on the _____ (brakes).

4. Explain that the omitted word can be discovered by saying the underlined parts of the words, then blending them together (brakes).
5. Repeat steps 1 to 4, using other words and sentences such as:

   <u>tr</u>ain   <u>gl</u>ass
   b<u>lade</u>   s<u>itter</u>

Have students discover the new word and then use it in a sentence.

Extended activities:

1. Have prepared sheet as shown in example. Students choose sentence the new word completes.

   bean   1. Let's sit on the ___ in the park.
   lun<u>ch</u>   2. The ___ is sandy.
           3. The ___ of grapes was purple.

2. On the chalkboard draw two big circles. Have words with phonetic parts underlined in each circle. Student picks a word from each circle, blends the underlined part, and writes the word on the chalkboard.

beat
<u>b</u>ay (other words)   m<u>eat</u> (other words)

SILENT LETTERS IN WORDS

Objective: The student will be able to identify the silent letter or letters on words.

Materials: flash cards containing words with and without silent letters

Procedure:

1. Prepare word cards with one word on each which may or may not have silent letters. If the word has a silent letter, write the letter on the back of the card.
2. Divide the students into two teams, giving each student a card.

3. A student from each team stands and faces a student from the other team, both holding their cards so the other can see. Each student identifies the silent letter or letters, if any, held by the other member.
4. Each correct identification wins one point for the team.

Extended activities:

1. Bring several newspapers to school. Each student or pair of students chooses an article and circles all the words in the article containing a silent letter. Then exchange articles and have students mark through all the silent letters in the circled words.
2. On the chalkboard write a list of words containing silent vowels or consonants:

> knew, gnaw, leaf, plate, light

Students copy the words and mark out the silent letter or letters.
3. Pass out ditto sheets with the following words and directions:

WORKSHEET

Circle the silent letter or letters in the words below:

(k) n e w	p l a t (e)
n i (g h) t	l i (g h) t
(g) n a w	e (a) s t
l e (a) f	c h (i) e f
g a (i) t	f u (d) g (e)

4. Have a box or bag with a letter such as "k" or silent letters written on it. Have students find pictures of objects that contain the silent letter to fill the box or bag. (See following page.)

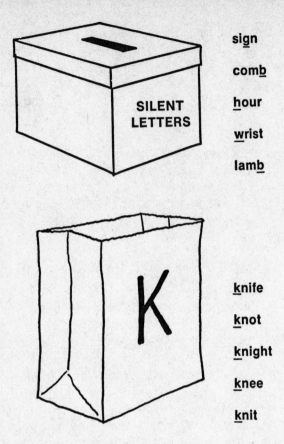

si**g**n

com**b**

hour

wrist

lam**b**

knife

knot

knight

knee

knit

Brief Review—Sound and Symbol Recognition (Phonics)

As you know, some students have better ears for phonic instruction than others. We suggest that if some students failed to grasp sound-symbol relationships, you check them for auditory discrimination ability. Auditory discrimination ability is thought to be a prerequisite to learning phonics. There are several commercially available tests which you could employ if you think it necessary. You should also keep in mind the fact that if some students fail to respond to sound instruction, your emphasis should shift to teaching other word recognition skills.

5

Increasing Structural Analysis Skills

If a reader fails to recognize an unknown word and cannot determine the word by using context clues, he or she should use structural analysis. Breaking a word into its parts to recognize affixes, roots, inflectional endings, etc., is using structural analysis to identify known parts which often provide the key to recognizing the multisyllabic word. And in this chapter, you have a rich resource of lesson plans enabling you to develop all the skills related to structural analysis.

Begin your instruction with any lesson in this chapter. If you have no particular priority, start with inflectional endings and do the four-part series of lesson plans. Continue next with whichever one you deem necessary. If not all students grasp your instruction after completing the lesson or lessons, you should come back to that skill at a later time. Repeat the lesson again or change words if you think it best, but remember—these are generic lessons which can be used again and again.

INFLECTED WORD ENDING (s)

Objective: Students will make use of inflected word forms by using in sentences words to which *s* endings have been added.

Materials: prepared worksheet for follow-up

Procedure:

1. Write on the board sentences such as: I <u>walk</u> to school. He <u>walks</u> to school. Ask a pupil to read the sentences aloud.
2. Then point to the word *walks* in the second sentence and say, "What ending is added to the word *walk*? Does adding *s* to the word *walk* mean more than one?"
3. Tell pupils that we say *I walk* but *he walks*.
4. Continue with the same procedure, using other known words such as *hands, pulls,* and *runs*.
5. Ask pupils to identify the root word in each.
6. Ask, "Does adding the *s* make the word mean more than one?"
7. On the chalkboard write sentences containing underlined inflected forms that can be used as either nouns or verbs:

> Jan <u>walks</u> to the store.
> You may sweep the <u>walks</u>.
> He <u>bats</u> with his left hand.
> Three <u>bats</u> are lost.

8. Have a child read each sentence, then ask, "In which sentence does the underlined word mean more than one?" Then ask, "What is the root word in each underlined word?"
9. Then write inflected forms of known words such as *pulls, hands, walks, bats*.
10. Ask, "When these words are not in sentences, can we tell whether they mean more than one?"
11. Lead pupils to discover that unless these words are used in sentences, it cannot be known whether they mean more than one.

Extended activity:

Distribute prepared worksheets to each pupil with sentences containing inflected forms of known words. Have pupils circle each underlined word that means more than one.

INFLECTED WORDS: Singular/Plural

Objective: Students will make use of inflected word forms in choosing regular or plural words or in matching singular or plural words with pictures.

Materials: —cards on which both singular and plural word forms are written
—picture cards that match words on the cards

Procedure:

1. Show pupils pictures in which there are single and plural objects. Lead pupils to use singular and plural word forms naturally as they are asked to tell what they see in the pictures. (These pictures may be placed on the chalk ledge or on a prepared worksheet for each pupil.)

2. Write the word "bug" on the board and have a pupil read the word aloud.
3. Write an *s* at the end of "bug" and have someone read "bugs" aloud. Say, "Do the two words sound different?" Lead the pupils to discover that the letter "s" was added and now the word has more sounds.
4. Have pupils point to pictures showing more than one object. Call attention to the word under the picture. Ask, "How are the words alike under pictures showing more than one thing?"
5. Use the same procedure to show plural words in which *es* is added to a root word (fish, dish, box, etc.).

Extended Activities:

Individuals or small groups may match word cards showing singular and plural forms to pictures of both singular and plural objects.

INFLECTED WORD ENDING (ed)

Objective: Students will use correct "ed" inflected word forms.

Materials: worksheet with sentences for follow-up

Procedures:

1. Place word cards for *looks* and *jumps* in the card holder.
2. Ask a pupil to read the words. Then have a pupil frame the root words and tell what ending was added to make *looks* and *jumps*.
3. Repeat the procedure with *looked* and *jumped*.
4. Write on the board the words *planted* and *hunted*.
5. Have a child underline the root word in each and read word.
6. Proceed with inflected words *splashed, jumped* and *played*.
7. Ask pupils to read the words, then ask, "Does the *ed* sound the same in each word?"

8. Say, "Sometimes the *ed* sounds as it does in *splashed*, sometimes as in *jumped*, and sometimes as in *played*.

Extended activity:

Distribute prepared worksheets on which sentences are written containing known roots to which *ed* is added. Have pupils underline roots in each:

1. Mary *showed* the box to me.
2. They *asked* for the cake.
3. Mr. Pig *painted* his house.
4. It *rained* all day.

INFLECTED WORD ENDING (ing)

Objective: Students will use inflected word forms by using in sentences words to which endings (*ing*) have been added.

Materials: prepared worksheet for follow-up

Procedures:

1. Write the word *talk* on the chalkboard and ask a pupil to read it.
2. Then add *ing* and ask a pupil to read the word *talking* and use it in a sentence.
3. Continue procedure with words such as *wish, sleep, stay,* and *pull.*
4. After pupils read root words, ask them to read the inflected form.
5. Have each root word used in an oral sentence and each inflected word form used in a sentence.

Extended activity:

Prepare and distribute worksheets such as the following and tell each pupil to write the word that completes each sentence.

WORKSHEET

1. The rabbit was _____ in the grass.
   jump   jumped   jumping

2. Stan was _____ the wagon.
   pull   pulled   pulling

3. Mr. Pig __ on the grass.
   walk   walked   walking

AFFIXES—PREFIXES

Objective: Given a list of words, students will identify and know
the meaning of the prefixes.

Procedure:

1. Write the following prefixed words on the board or use a transparency on the overhead projector: discover, invisible, unseen, regain, immovable, postseason, pregame, deface.
2. Ask students to look for familiar words within these words. Point out the root words are preceded by prefixes which change the meanings.
3. Have students determine what each root word and prefix is, such as de and face for deface.
4. Select students to look up each prefix in their dictionaries.
5. Ask students to decide what each root means.
6. Have students put the meaning of each root with the definition of each prefix and determine if the meaning of the root word changes.
7. Have students use each new word in a complete sentence.

AFFIXES—SUFFIXES

Objective: Given a list of words, students will identify and know
the meaning of the suffixes.

Procedure:

1. Write the following suffixed words on the board or use the overhead projector: glossy, helper, temptation, quietness, ornamental, blameless, actor, homeward.
2. Ask students to look for familiar words within these words. Point out that the root words are followed by suffixes which change the meaning or function.
3. Have students determine what each root word and suffix is, such as gloss and y for *glossy*.
4. Pick students to look up each suffix in their dictionaries.
5. Ask students to decide what each root means.
6. Have students put the meaning of each root with the definition of each suffix and determine if the meaning of the root word changes.
7. Have students use each new word in a complete sentence.

POSSESSIVES (Singular Form)

Objective: Students will identify correctly singular possessive noun forms.

Procedure:

1. On the chalkboard, write your name and the name of the students in the group. Talk about everyone having something that belongs to him or her and ask the students to think about something that is their very own.
2. Beside your name write the name of something belonging to you. Have students tell about the object they own and write it on the chalkboard beside their names.
3. Discuss and demonstrate that the way to show ownership when writing or reading is by adding an *'s* to the end of the name, using your name as an example.
4. Have the students add the *'s* to their name and read it:

   Bob's bike.

5. Using your name and ownership object, make a sentence:

   "Mrs. McGregor's dog is at home."

   Write the sentence on the chalkboard.
6. Ask for volunteers to make sentences using their name and ownership object. Write these on the chalkboard.
7. Discuss each sentence as follows:

   Bill's hat was lost.

   Ask: To whom does the hat belong? Underline the word that tells whose hat it is.

   What was added to Bill's name to show that it was his hat?

8. Lead students to realize that each example had only one owner.

Extended activities:

1. Have students copy some or all (according to the size of the group) of the sentences used in the lesson, underlining the word showing ownership:

   <u>Bill's</u> hat was lost.

2. Students can create their own sentences using members of the class or their families.

3. Have students rewrite phrases to show ownership:

   uncle   farm   —uncle's farm
   mother   book   —mother's book

4. Have students match the correct possessive form:

   Mary   Bill's
                pencil   bike
   Mary's   Bill

   Tony
                book
   Tony's

POSSESSIVES (Plural Form)

Objective: Students will identify the correct endings of phrases containing plural possessive forms.

Procedures:

1. Write a known word on the chalkboard, such as *cow*. Discuss or review how the possessive of one noun is shown by adding an *'s*. Write *cow's* on chalkboard.
2. Ask for the plural form of *cow* by saying, "How would you write *cow* if there were more than one *cow*?" Write *cows* on the chalkboard.
3. Say, "If there were three cows that the sugar belonged to, we would do this." (Now illustrate by adding the apostrophe *after* the *s*.)
4. Continue using other examples. Make sure the plural form of the word requires only an *s*—girl, father, book, farmer, moon.
5. Ask a volunteer to explain the difference between making a singular word and a plural word possessive. (Add an *'s* to make a singular word show possession. If an *'s* has been added to make the plural of the word add only the apostrophe after the *s*.)
6. Now write the word *child* on the board and discuss the meaning of the word and how to form the possessive by adding *'s*. Ask, "How would you change the word to mean more than one child?" Write *children* on the chalkboard. Lead students to realize no *s* has been added.
7. Write *party* after *children*. Ask how you would show that the party belongs to the children. (Add *'s*.)
8. Continue with other words: start with the singular form; show possessive form of singular; make word plural; show possessive form of plural:

Singular	Possessive	Plural	Plural Possessive
spy	spy's	spies	spies'
hero	hero's	heroes	heroes'

Singular	Possessive	Plural	Plural Possessive
man	man's	men	men's
sheep	sheep's	sheep	sheep's
ox	ox's	oxen	oxen's
horse	horse's	horses	horses'

9. Have students group the words in the final plural possessive column according to those which required an *'s* and those which required only an ':

's	'
men's	spies'
sheep's	heroes'
oxen's	horses'

10. Ask for a volunteer to make up a rule for showing possession or ownership. (If an *s* was added to a word to make it plural add only an apostrophe. If the plural form does not end in *s,* add the *'s*).

Extended activities:

1. Have words in random order for students to group under correct heading:

spoon	woman's	forms	women's
babies	cup	toys	daisy's
churches'	bottles'	apron	house's

Singular	Possessive	Plural	Plural Possessive
spoon	woman's	forms	women's
apron	daisy's	babies	churches'
cup	house's	toys	bottles'

2. Have more words for students to change from singular to possessive, to plural, to plural possessive:

Singular	Possessive	Plural	Plural Possessive
butterfly	butterfly's	butterflies	butterflies'
orchard	orchard's	orchards	orchards'

Singular	Possessive	Plural	Plural Possessive
fox	fox's	foxes	foxes'
knife	knife's	knives	knives'

ADJECTIVAL RECOGNITION

Objective: Students will be able to distinguish between positive, comparative and superlative adjectives.

Materials: none

Procedure:

1. Write the words "good," "better," "best" on the board.
2. Ask the students, "If _____'s (student's name) mother baked a *good* cake, would you want a piece of it?"
3. Ask the students, "If _____'s mother made a better cake than _____'s (first student's name) mother, which cake would you rather have a piece of?"
4. Now ask students, "If _____'s mother made the best cake in the neighborhood, would you rather have a piece of her cake, or a piece of cake that someone else in the neighborhood made?"
5. Discuss the difference between the words "good," "better," and "best."
6. Ask students what kind of words "good," "better," and "best" are.
7. After you have established that these words are adjectives, tell students that these words differ in that they describe different degrees of the quality they describe as adjectives. Explain that if a piece of cake tastes "good," it is tasty. If we say that another piece of cake is "better" than the first, we have compared the two pieces of cake, and determined that one is "more good" than the other. Say that we do not say "more good," but we say (what?). Students should shout, "Better!"
8. Explain that we have names for adjectives that describe things in varying degrees. Write the word "positive" under the word

"good," the word "comparative" under the word "better," and the word "superlative" under the word "best."

9. Ask students to think of other examples of positives, comparatives and superlatives.
10. Write the words on the board, labeling each as positive, comparative or superlative at the student's direction as you go.

PREPOSITIONAL PHRASES

Objective: Students will identify the meaning of selected prepositional phrases.

Materials: phrase strips

Procedure:

1. Display phrases on sentence strips such as:

   <u>in his yard</u>   <u>at the moon</u>   <u>with his toys</u>

2. Say: "One of these phrases is made up of words that tell where Stan may play when he is home."
3. Ask a pupil to read the phrase aloud.
4. Say: "One of the phrases has the word *moon* in it. Who can read the phrase?"
5. Now read the phrase with *toys* in it.
6. Write sentences such as the ones below, and have pupils supply the phrase that completes the sentences.

   1. Stan likes to play _____.
   2. It was night and he looked _____.
   3. Then he went inside _____.

7. Continue procedure, using other sentences and phrases at intervals or as new words are presented.

Extended activity:

Prepare and distribute an exercise similar to the one at the top of the facing page. Have pupils read the first part of the sentence and then underline all the phrases that will complete the sentence.

Bill went	to the store
	had a candy cane
	after the big balloon
The birds went	into the nest
	likes to play
	after a bug
Mark had	on a new jacket
	on his hat
	went away
The stars were	in the sky
	at the pond
	on the hill

PRONOUNS

Objective: Students will recognize and understand pronouns.

Materials: word cards containing pronouns and a prepared chart as illustrated in follow-up activity

Procedure:

1. Write pairs of sentences on the chalkboard, such as:

    1. This is John's jacket. *It* is good to play in.
    2. "Look at the candle," said Jack. "I can jump over it."

2. Have a pupil read the first pair of sentences.
3. Point out the word *it* in the second sentence. Explain that the word it stands for is a word in the first sentence.
4. Ask, "Which word in the first sentence does *it* stand for?" Call for a student to underline the word.
5. Repeat the procedure for the other pairs of sentences using *it*.

Extended activity:

A.   On large chart paper or poster board fasten 12 (more or less) library card pockets. On each pocket attach a picture (which can be easily changed) of a group of boys; girls; cars; bugs; a boy; a girl; a pencil; etc. Give the pupils word cards on each of which has been written a pronoun. Have pupils place the cards with the pronoun *it* in the correct pockets.

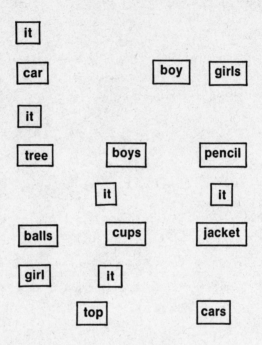

Use same activity for presentation of other pronouns.

B.   Present pronouns *we, us, them, they*.

1. Write sentences on chalkboard, such as:

—The dog and horse ran after Jane and me.
—Mike and Pat helped the bird back into the nest.
—Mark and Kim went to the zoo.
—Pam and John had cake for Jan and me.
—Mary and I played with the Frisbee.

2. Have a pupil read the first sentence and ask: "Which words can be replaced by one of the pronouns? Which one of the pronouns?"

3. Ask a pupil to erase the words *Jan and me* and substitute *us*.
4. Continue the same procedure with the other sentences.

CONTRACTIONS

Objective: Students will demonstrate their awareness that certain letters are omitted and replaced by an apostrophe in forming contractions.

Materials: —crayon
                   —scissors
                   —glue
                   —construction paper
                   —worksheet described in follow-up activity 2

Procedure:

1. Distribute to students a list of words which can be combined with the word "not" to form contractions. On the list have as many "nots" as you have words:

have	not
do	not
did	not
should	not

   Words should be printed very large on this list.
2. Direct students to form contractions by cutting away the extra letters and gluing the new words to their construction paper.
3. Have children use the crayon to add the apostrophe in place of the missing letters.
4. After all new words have been glued on paper, have children read their new words, and tell what two words they were made from.
5. Ask students to use these words in original sentences.

Extended activities:

1. Put sentences on the board with the two words used rather than the contraction, and have students replace the two words with a contraction.
2. Distribute a worksheet of sentences, omitting a contraction. Students fill in the blanks:

> Mary _____ play ball. (can't)
> Dad _____ like roses. (doesn't)
> Jan _____ swim. (won't)
> He _____ get up from his sick bed. (shouldn't)
> Henry _____ in school today. (isn't)
> Come to think of it, Bill _____ been here all day. (hasn't)
> Jim _____ run the 100-yard dash under ten seconds. (can't)
> Over the hill, _____ clustered together. (they're)
> All ready it is ten _____ this morning. (o'clock)

COMPOUND WORDS

Objectives: 1. Students will understand that a word formed by putting together two or more words is called a compound word.
2. The children will be able to use the clues in sentences to write compound words to complete the sentences.
3. The children will be able to identify the compound words represented by pictures.

Materials: —worksheet for lesson
—construction paper
—crayons
—newsprint for follow-up activities

Procedure:

1. Guide the children through the following questions:

a. What do you call a man made from snow?
b. What do you call a ball made from snow?
c. What words are put together to make these words?
d. Can you think of other compound words?

2. Discuss whether or not the meanings of the separate words were changed when the words were put together. Discuss the separate meanings and the new meanings.
3. Direct your students to look at the following sentences and use the clues in the sentences to write compound words to complete the sentences.

a. A book that helps Mother to cook is a ———.
b. A ball that players throw through a basket is a ———.
c. A coat that you wear in the rain is a ———.
d. A cage for a bird is a ———.
e. A hook used for catching fish is a ———.
f. A house with a light on top is a ———.
g. The room in which a bed is kept is a ———.
h. The yard of a church is a ———.

4. Explain that you have some compound words that have lost their partners. Have the children help you add the word needed to make them compound words again:

fire ———	——— bird
———plane	snow———
sun———	———ache
———light	butter———
rail———	———boy
———melon	fisher———
ever———	———walk

5. Provide worksheet of pictures only (page 120) to each pupil. Have each pupil write a compound word for each of the pictures.

Extended activities:

1. Provide your students a piece of 12" x 18" colored construction paper. Draw a very light line in the middle. Fold both outside edges in to touch pencil line, as sketched at top of page 121.

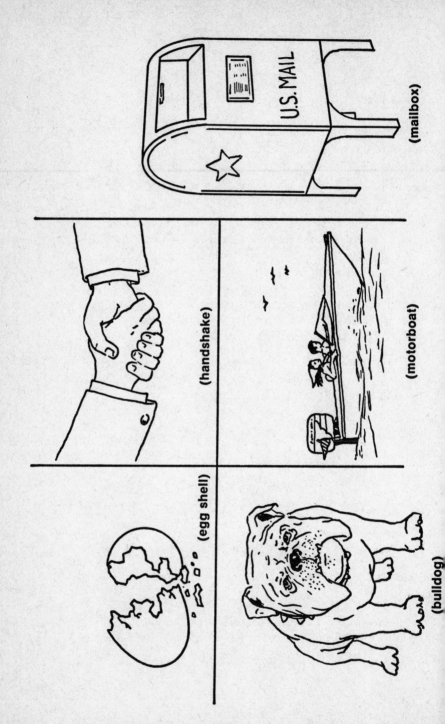

(mailbox)

(handshake)

(motorboat)

(egg shell)

(bulldog)

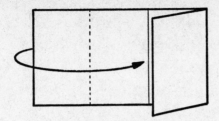

This forms a "booklet" which opens to the width of the full page. Instruct students to "close up" the booklet and write on the outside.

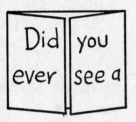

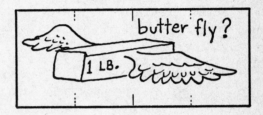

Each student chooses a compound word that creates a funny picture when the two words are separate:

milkshake	hatband	iceskate
eardrum	catfish	windmill
horsefly	lunchbox	sawmill

2. Game: Divide your group into two teams. A team member from Team I goes to the board and writes the first part of a compound word of which he is thinking. A member of Team II goes to the board and finishes the word. If it is the word the first child had in mind, Team II gets two points; if the answer is a compound word but not the intended word, one point. If the Team II member thinks the word is not a correct word, he challenges; the word is looked up. If it is not a word, Team II gets 3 points; if it is a word, Team I gets 3 points.

3. Have your students fold a piece of newsprint into eight sections. They may draw in each section a picture of a compound word

they know. Have the picture cut apart, and place everyone's pictures in the same box. Take the pictures out one at a time. The one who extracts a picture tells the compound word it represents.

ROOT WORDS

Objective: Students will be able to identify root words in the context of the word formed with the root word.

Materials: three scramble cube word games

Procedure:

1. Write the word "preview" on the board.
2. Discuss the meaning of the word with students.
3. Emphasize the importance of the word "view" in giving the word "preview" its meaning. Circle "view" within "preview" on the board.
4. Write the word "awaken" on the board. Ask if anyone sees a word that gives meaning to the word "awaken" within that word. When students have established that "wake" is a word within "awaken" that gives it meaning, ask if anyone knows what we call a word within a multisyllable word that gives the word its meaning.
5. Write "root word" on the board. Emphasize that a root word is the main word within a multisyllable word that gives that word its meaning.
6. Ask students to suggest other words that are made from root words. Write the words on the board as students suggest them.
7. After you have three or four words on the board and you feel that students have grasped the concept, divide the class into three or four small groups. Give each group some scramble cube word games, and tell them to make as a group as many words with root words as they can, and write the words down as they make them with the scramble cube letter blocks, then circle the root word

within each word, as they saw you do on the board with the word "preview." At the end of 15 minutes, total up how many words each group was able to make.

VERBS: Irregular Agreement with Subject

Objective: Students will be able to recognize and use different forms of irregular verbs.

Materials none

Procedure:

1. Write the following sentences on the board:

   > I can type.
   > The secretary typed a letter.
   > She types well.

2. Review the base form of the verb, the present and past tenses, using these sentences as examples.
3. Write the following sentences on the board:

   > I can grow flowers from seeds.
   > The flower grows taller every day.
   > We grew our own tomatoes this year.

4. Ask students which is the base form of the verb, the present tense, and the past tense.
5. Ask students what the difference in the past tense of the verbs "type" and "grow" is.
6. After discussion, explain that verbs that form their past tense with "ed" are regular verbs. Add that verbs that form their past tense with a "t" or a "d" are also regular verbs. State that verbs that do not form their past tense in this way, such as "grow," which in the past tense becomes "grew," are called irregular verbs.
7. Ask students to think of verbs and classify them as either regular

or irregular, making a column for each type on the board, and writing them down in present and past form as the students call them out.

VERBS: Tense Usage

Objective: Students will be able to use the correct form of verbs in the context of sentences.

Materials: none

Procedure:

1. Write the following sentences on the board:

    I talk with my firends.
    Today Betty talks with her friends.
    Yesterday Betty talked her mother into taking her to the movies.

2. Ask students to identify the subject and verb in each sentence.
3. After students have identified subjects and verbs in each sentence, ask them why we used the verb "talk" in the first sentence, "talks" in the second sentence, and "talked" in the third.
4. After discussion, emphasize that "talk" is the base form of the verb, "talks" is the present tense, and "talked" is the past tense.
5. Write the words *base, present,* and *past* beside the words "talk," "talks," and "talked" on the board in the following manner:

    talk—base
    talks—present
    talked—past

6. Explain that the base form is the verb itself and is used when

making a general descriptive statement with the verb, such as "I talk with my friends." Point out that the sentence is a general statement and that no specific time is implied.

7. Explain that the present tense of the verb "talk" is "talks." This verb describes action or an event that takes place in the present, right now, as, "Today Betty talks with her friends."

8. Explain that the past tense of the verb "talk" is "talked" and is used to describe an action or event that took place in the past, as in the sentence, "Yesterday Betty talked her mother into taking her to the movies."

9. Emphasize that we call the different verb forms tenses. Explain that tenses are the different forms of verbs used to specify the time space in which the action or event described takes place.

10. Write the word "walk" on the board.

11. Tell students that "walk" is the base form of this word.

12. Ask students to make a sentence with "walk."

13. Write the sentence, "Today she ____ to school, " on the board.

14. Ask students to fill in the blank with the present tense of the verb "walk."

15. Write the sentence, "Yesterday I ____ three miles," on the board.

16. Ask students to fill in the past tense of the verb "walk."

17. Emphasize to students that the verb in a sentence must be the correct tense to fit structurally into the sentence with the subject. State that we say that the verb agrees with the subject when they fit together correctly in this manner.

NOUNS AND VERBS (Distinguishing Between)

Objective: By using verbs and nouns properly in sentences, students will demonstrate their ability to distinguish between them

Materials: two ditto sheets and a pencil for each student

Procedure:

1. Discuss orally with the students what verbs are. Describe verbs as "doing" words, or "action" words that are used in sentences.
2. Give several examples of verbs in sentences:

    Please <u>drink</u> your milk, Thomas.
    The ant <u>walked</u> across the leaf.
    A small brown rabbit <u>jumped</u> into the bushes.

3. Describe nouns as the names of people, places or things; explain that they are what or who is doing something in the sentence.
4. Use the same sentences above to illustrate nouns.
5. Hand out dittos to the students.
6. Ask the students to put an *x* by the words that are verbs.
7. Tell the students to fill in the sentences using the list of words above the sentences.
8. Allow the students 15 to 20 minutes.

WORKSHEET

Put an *x* by the verbs in this list. Put an *o* by the nouns in this list.

__jumping	__goat	__kick	__sky
__walk	__stand	__hide	__room
__ride	__bicycle	__laugh	__jungle
__newspaper	__tree	__plant	__read

Fill in the following sentences, using the words above in the proper spaces.

1. John can _____ the ball 20 feet!
2. The bright _____ had only a few small clouds in it.
3. The _____ was _____ over the fence.
4. We _____ at funny jokes.
5. Did you _____ the _____ want-ads this morning?
6. We always _____ quietly in the lunch line.
7. The _____ was filled with wild animals and snakes!
8. You can't ride your _____ if it has a broken spoke.
9. This spring we will _____ corn, beans and peas in the garden.
10. The giant oak _____ was shattered when the lightning hit it.

Extended activities:

1. Have the students invent their own sentences, in which the rest of the class must find the verbs and nouns.
2. Have the students play charades, using action words for the answer to the charade.

PHRASE MEANING

Objective: The student will comprehend phrases that tell *who, what, when, where, why,* and *how* in sentence parts.

Materials: several pictures and cards on which the question words are written

Procedure:

1. Tell the students you are going to say phrases or parts of sentences. Explain that the phrases will tell *who, what, when, why, where,* or *how.*
2. Say several phrases for each question word. Have students state the phrase word that explains the phrase:

    > because he was hungry (why)
    > a glass of water (what)
    > tomorrow when)
    > by running quickly (how)
    > under the tree (where)
    > a man (who)

3. Show students a picture. Pass out the cards containing the question word.
4. Ask students to hold up their card if it tells about the phrase you say.

in the pond (<u>where</u>)

the turtles (<u>who</u>)

under the tree (<u>where</u>)

swam (<u>what</u>)

because it was hot (<u>why</u>)

5. Repeat steps 3 and 4, using other pictures.

Extended activity A:

1. Have students read a story, then find the phrases that tell *who*, *what*, *when*, *where*, *why*, and *how*.
2. Have students write a list of phrases or words telling *who*, *what*, *when*, *where*, *why*, and *how*:

Who?	What?	When?
a boy	ran down the tree	at 10 o'clock
mother	fell into the water	today

Where?	Why?	How?
at school	because he fell	quickly
beside the bed	because they were tired	as fast as you can

Extended activity B:

Materials: phrase cards, card holder

Procedure:

1. Write on the chalkboard the following headings:

   when   where   what   why   how

2. Then distribute phrase cards with phrases such as:

at first	before dark	out of the house
a yellow flower	many trees	in a blue dress
very fast	over the roof	this morning
after the ride	in the blue house	today
	on the baby	to eat

3. As each pupil is called, he or she writes the phrase on the chalkboard under the appropriate heading.
4. After all phrases have been categorized have the pupils read the phrases aloud.

Extended activity C:

1. Repeat the procedure, using other phrases and the same headings.
2. This activity may be done on an individual basis, using a card holder for the headings and place phrases in the holder under appropriate heading.

IDENTIFICATION OF SENTENCE PARTS

Objective: After hearing an unfamiliar story, and reading one, the student will be able to recall details by answering *who, what, when, where, why,* and *how* questions.

Materials: two unfamiliar stories on student's reading level

Procedure:

1. Read an unfamiliar story to the students.
2. Ask students *who, what, when, where, why,* and *how* questions such as:

> "Who is the story about?"
> "What did the person do?"
> "Why did he do it?"
> "Where did this happen?"
> "Why did it happen?"
> "How did it happen?"

Use as many stories as needed for understanding.
3. Have students read a selection from an unfamiliar source.
4. Ask questions containing *who, what, when, where, why, how.*

Extended activities:

1. Read a story to the class or have students read a story. Then have students draw pictures to illustrate the parts of the story that told *who, what, where, why, when, how*?

WHO?   WHAT?   WHERE?
WHY?   WHEN?   HOW?

2. Game: Divide class into teams or call on individuals. Ask a student to give as much information as he can about a given word or subject. One point is received for each fact:

scallop—Scallop is a noun.
       It has two syllables.
       It has five consonants.
       It has two vowels.
       It is spelled s-c-a-l-l-o-p.
       It is edible.

       (6 points)

PUNCTUATION: Scrambled Sentences

Objectives: Given scrambled sentences, the pupils will be able to:
       (a) rearrange the words into a sentence.
       (b) write the sentences.
       (c) begin the sentence with a capital letter and end the sentence with a period.

Materials: —tagboard strips with nouns, verbs, and prepositional phrases.
       —writing paper
       —drawing paper
       —pencil and crayons

Procedure:

1. Talk about the pupils' school experiences: things they do in school, people they have met at school, and things they have learned in school.
2. Using the tagboard strips arrange the three elements in scrambled fashion. Call on a pupil to rearrange the elements to make a sentence.

(a) prepositional phrases:

on the bike	up the steps
in the bed	to the show
at home	into the water

(b) nouns:

she	they
he	we
the pup	a cat

(c) verbs:

rode	ran
sat	walked
went	were

2. Write the following sentences about school on the board and have the students tell you how to write them correctly.

   a. sing we to like
   b. likes paint to he
   c. work like to we
   d. pals have school in we
   e. go we school to like to

4. Stress that the sentences begin with capital letters and end with punctuation.

Extended activities:

1. Take five sentences from the pupils' reading lessons, scramble the words and write them on the board. Have the children make sentences of them and write them on paper, using capitals and periods.
2. Have the pupils draw themselves doing the thing they like best to do in school. Allow the children to share their pictures.

QUOTATIONS

Objective: Pupils show skill in punctuating sentences in which the speaker is identified before a direct quotation.

Materials: —comic section of newspaper or a comic book
                —a worksheet as described in Follow-up Activity #2

Procedure:

1. Write sentences containing quotations on the board:

   > Bill said, "Have a piece of cake."
   > Dad asked, "Are we going to the movie?"

2. Explain which part of each sentence gives someone's exact words.
3. Stress the point that "quotation" refers to the exact words of the speaker. Point out that *Bill said* and *Dad asked* are words that are not being actually spoken.
4. Point out that the quotation could stand alone and requires the same capitalization and punctuation regardless of the quotation marks.
5. Allude to a cartoon strip of a comic book to show the relationship of quotation marks to the encircled spoken phrases depicted coming from the mouth of a character. Draw figure on the chalkboard.

Extended activities:

1. Have students find and write sentences from a story they have read in which the speaker is identified before a direct quotation.
2. Make worksheet with several sentences in which the speaker is identified before the quotation, but omit punctuation. Have pupils put in punctuation:

> Mother said Go to sleep!
> At the PTA Father stated First priority is education.
> Bobby read the book and happily reported This is the best
> book I have ever read.
> While laughing at themselves Pete and Repete uttered Sorry
> we goofed.

NUMBER OF SYLLABLES
(Auditory-Visual)

Objective: Given multisyllabic words, students will demonstrate their ability to identify the correct number or syllables.

Procedure:

1. Write two known words on the chalkboard, such as: *care — careless*.
2. Pronounce the words, tapping out the syllables on a hard surface. Emphasize the syllables.
3. Ask, "How many times did I tap for the word *care*? *careless*?"
4. Explain that the taps help us to know how many syllables are in a word.
5. Talk about the number of vowels seen in the word *care*, then about how many are heard.
6. Repeat step 5 with the word *careless*.
7. Write other familiar one- and two-syllable words on the chalkboard. Have pupils tap out the syllables as the words are pronounced. Call attention to the number of vowels seen and heard.

8. Say other words without writing them. Have them tap out the syllables.
9. Say words with one and two syllables. Have pupils write the number indicating how many syllables heard.

Extended activities:

1. Write known one- and two-syllable words on chalkboard. Have pupils write the one-syllable words in one column and the two-syllable words in another column.
2. Write sentences such as the following on the chalkboard. Have pupils complete the incomplete word by supplying the missing syllable:

> John walked swift ——— to the store.
> Be care——— when us——— matches.
> I will be glad when the cir——— comes.

VCCV PRINCIPLE (Vowel, Consonant, Consonant, Vowel)

Objective: Students will apply the rule that if the first vowel in a polysyllabic word is followed by two consonants, the first syllable ends with the first of the two consonants and the vowel sound is usually short.

Procedure:

1. In a column on the chalkboard write familiar two-syllable words containing the VCCV pattern, such as: *contain.*
2. Point to each word and pronounce it, slightly emphasizing the two syllables. Explain that saying it slowly will help you hear the syllables.
3. Ask pupils where the first syllable ended. Draw a slash mark (/) between the syllables. Do this for each word.
4. Lead pupils to see that the first vowel in each word is followed

by two consonants and that the first consonant ends the first syllable.

5. List several words in which the first vowel is followed by two
like consonants, such as *little, rabbit.* Call attention to the double
consonants following the first vowel. Lead pupils to note that in
each word the first syllable ends with the first of the two consonants. Remind pupils that the second *like* consonant is silent.
6. Ask pupils to decide the sound of the first vowel in each word,
then ask why the vowel has that sound. (See lesson for syllable
and vowel principle under Vowel Principles.)

Extended activities:

1. Have sentences containing VCCV words. Have pupils underline the VCCV words, divide them into syllables, and mark the
first vowel in each word:

   The family went on a pĭc/nic.

2. Make a list of words with double consonants. Have pupils divide
the word using a slash mark, cross out the silent consonant, and
mark the sound of the first vowel:

   răb/b̶it

VCV PRINCIPLE (Vowel, Consonant, Vowel)

Objective: The students will understand the principle of the place-
ment of the vowel in an open and closed syllable.

Materials: none

Procedure:

1. Write familiar words in two columns on the chalkboard. For the
first column select words in which the first syllable ends with the
vowel, such as *paper, motel, local, laden, minor.* In the second
column use words in which the first syllable ends with the consonant, such as *robin, never, liver, livid, mimic.*

2. Have words in the first column pronounced and ask pupils to decide where the first syllable should end. Tell pupils that if they say the word slowly they can tell where it should be divided. Draw a slash mark (/) between the syllables and ask pupils to decide the division point.
3. Lead pupils to see that there is only one consonant after the first vowel and that in these words it begins the second syllable. Note that the vowel is at the end of the first syllable and the sound is long.
4. Repeat step 2 with the second column of words.
5. Lead pupils to see that these words also have one consonant after the first vowel, but the consonant ends the first syllable. Call attention to the first vowel. In these words it is short because it is followed by a consonant. (See lesson syllables and vowel principles under Vowel Principles.)
6. Have pupils compare words in both columns. Note that all words in both columns have the VCV pattern. Explain that with this pattern the first syllable can end either with the first vowel or with the consonant after the first vowel. Saying it slowly will help determine where the syllable ends.

Extended activity:

Have a list of familiar words using the VCV pattern. They should be mixed according to the division. Have students divide the syllables with a slash mark (/), then mark the first vowel:

ho̅/tel   măg/ic

SYLLABLES AND VOWEL PRINCIPLES

Objective: Students will demonstrate their ability in applying long and short vowel generalizations based on position in syllables.

Procedure:

1. Write a list of familiar one-syllable words on the chalkboard.
2. Have pupils pronounce each word, telling whether the sound of the vowel is long or short.
3. Lead them to understand that if there is only one vowel in a word and the vowel begins the word or is in the middle of the word, the vowel is usually short. Ask questions such as: "How many vowels do you see?" "Where is the vowel?"
4. Write on the chalkboard two columns of two-syllable words—one column of words whose first syllable ends with a vowel, such as: *ho tel, ra dio, my self, be hind, pi lot;* and another column of words whose first syllable ends in a consonant, such as: *af ter, sim ple, cir cus, box es, pen cil, suc ker.* Separate the syllables with a space.
5. Have pupils read aloud each word in the first column. Ask which vowel is seen, its sound, and its position in the word.
6. Lead students to understand that when a vowel comes at the end of a syllable, the sound it represents is usually long.
7. Repeat step 5, using the second column.
8. Lead pupils to generalize that vowels appearing at the beginning or middle of a syllable are usually short.

Extended activities:

Write a column of two-syllable words on the chalkboard. (Some examples are below.) Separate the syllables by a space. Have the two principles developed in the lesson written and numbered. Pupils write by each word the principle number which applies:

1. The vowel is usually short in a word or syllable if the vowel is at the beginning or middle.
2. The vowel is usually long in a word or syllable if the vowel is at the end.

    Example: ti ger 2   un der 1

( ) cat sup   ( ) ba con

( ) p<u>a</u>t   ( ) s<u>i</u>m   ple
( ) s<u>a</u>   vor   ( ) m<u>o</u>   tel
( ) m<u>o</u>n   key   ( ) p<u>a</u>   trol
( ) p<u>a</u>ck   age   ( ) s<u>u</u>m   mer
( ) h<u>i</u>t   ( ) <u>a</u>p   ple

Brief Review—Structural Analysis

As you have seen, this chapter on structural analysis skills is
extensive. Reteaching these lessons for review or additional instruction would be in your students' interests. Simply substitute examples and you have new lesson plans for reinforcing the skills your
students need. Occasional review is necessary for skill maintenance
even for your quick-to-learn students; therefore, until skills become
overlearned, schedule reviews—particularly of the more difficult
skills in this chapter such as verbs, possessives, and punctuation.

6

Enlarging Literal Comprehension Skills

Before students can become competent in understanding literal meanings, they must be able to recall details, understand sequence and analyze the story setting. These skills are well covered in this chapter. For example, understanding sequence is a progressively difficult skill to learn. Therefore, we have arranged a series of three lessons, each with extended activities, for the development of this skill. Beginning readers or readers who have difficulty understanding sequence should receive initial sequence instruction through "Sensible Sequence," which requires the ability to reorder a sequence of pictures. The second lesson deals with recalling specific parts in which an event or action occurred. The third and highest level of sequence skill development is understanding sequence of events, and the third lesson focuses on this. Thus, you have a stepping-stone approach to the development of a rather difficult literal comprehension skill. By moving from the simple to the complex, you will implement the best strategy for success with your students.

SENSIBLE SEQUENCE

Objective: Given a mixed series of pictures, the student will be able to arrange the series in logical order.

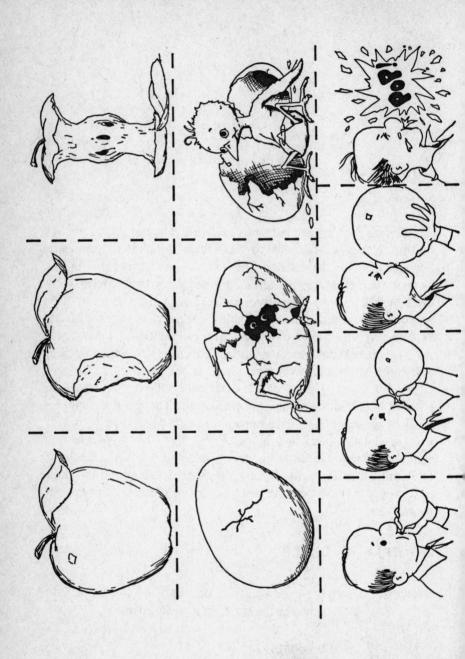

Materials: three series of three or four pictures as illustrated

Procedure:

1. Tell children that you are going to do some things. They are to watch carefully and try to tell you what you did. First, open the door to the closet containing your coat; next, put the coat on; last, close the closet door. (Any similar, simple, three-step sequence will serve.)
2. Ask the children to describe each of the things you did. After the events have been elicited in correct sequence, repeat them by introducing the words "first," "next," "last." "What did I do first?" (Opened door.) "Next?" (Put on coat.) "Last?" (Closed door.) Have children say "first," "next," "last."
3. Tell children that now, instead of watching someone do things, they are going to look at some pictures that show things happening. Present the three groups of sequence cards one group at a time. Ask which picture should come first, next, and last in each group. Be sure children can explain why.
4. Scramble the cards in each sequence and invite children to tell the story and arrange the cards in correct sequence.
5. Summarize lesson.

Extended activities:

1. Have students pantomime a task and have other students guess what they are doing.
2. Provide comic strips (cut apart) and have students arrange them in order as to what happened first, next, and last. Have numbers on back for self-checking.

SEQUENCE OF EVENTS—Parts

Objective: The student will recall the sequence of events by indicating the specific part of a story in which an event or action occurred.

Materials: two sets of identical sentence strips containing five sentences from a story the students have read

Procedure:

1. Select two groups of five children each.
2. Give each group a set of the prepared sentences in scrambled order.
3. Have each group member take one sentence.
4. Tell the group members to arrange themselves in a sequential order that makes a paragraph.

Extended activity:

Give students enough sentences for two paragraphs, along with the paragraph title. Instruct students to place the sentences in sequence on a card holder.

What We Did at School

- We saluted the flag.
- We had reading.
- Mr. Joyner taught us music.
- Math time was next.
- At 11:00 we had lunch.
- After a story, we studied birds.
- We wrote a story about birds.
- We got ready to go home.

UNDERSTANDING SEQUENCE OF EVENTS

Objective: The student will recall a series of events from written material by choosing the correct relationship of an event to other events in the material.

Materials: copies of "Making Ice Cream" story and multiple choice questions about story, given below

WORKSHEET
MAKING ICE CREAM

Making ice cream was always one of the most pleasurable summer events. It wasn't something that we did too often, so my brother Jack and I were always ready to do our share. Usually the first hint that we'd have of the afternoon's activity would be Dad's or Mom's low suggestion, "You think anyone would like some ice cream?" Quietly, we'd wait, looking from one to the other, watching for the nod of the head or quick smile that signaled agreement between them. Once the signal was given off we'd scatter, each to do our share of the work involved in making the creamy summer treat.

Dad's job was to get the ice cream churn off the high shelf in the kitchen pantry. Mom would begin to put together the cream, sugar, eggs and fruit in a smooth heavy mixture. Meanwhile, Jack and I would ride our bikes over to the Quick Stop store on Second Street and buy the bags of crushed ice we'd need to make the creamy mixture freeze. Carefully we'd wrap the ice in the canvas bags we'd carried with us and then we'd ride home as fast as we could. Once we were back home, all the supplies were ready. Now the hard work would begin.

Mother would carefully pour the heavy mixture of eggs, cream, sugar and fruit into the churn can. Then the dasher, or the mixing paddle, was pushed into place, the top added and firmly locked into place. Carefully all of this would be placed in the ice cream freezer. Dad would turn the crank for a couple of minutes. After making sure that everything was in place and the mixture well blended. Dad would add the layers of crushed ice and rock salt needed to freeze the mixture in the can. Now it was time for Jack and me to do our part.

Happy and enthusiastic, Jack and I would begin taking turns working the crank handle. At first, it was a lot of fun. The mixture was thin and turning the crank was easy. Later, after the cream began to thicken and freeze, the crank was harder to turn. We'd have to push harder and harder to keep the can moving and the paddle turning. Our arms, not used to the heavy strain, would begin to tire and hurt with each new effort. Of course, every so often, Dad would add more ice and salt to the freezer can and that break would give us just enough rest to allow us to keep on with the job.

Finally it would happen. The mixture in the can would become so stiff we couldn't turn the crank at all. Carefully, Dad would pour off the briny mixture of salt and melted ice that surrounded the mixing can. Once that was all drained off, he would layer new ice and salt around the can to ripen or freeze the ice cream in the mixing can. A large heavy towel was draped over the top and the whole thing set aside in the shade while the ice cream ripened.

At first the wait wasn't too bad. Jack and I welcomed the chance to rest our tired, aching arms. Usually we'd stretch out under a shady tree and make all kinds of plans about future adventures. Dad or Mom, or sometimes both of them, would sit with us and we'd hear their stories about our family and things that had happened long ago. But our thoughts never really strayed from the freezer ripening close by, and anxiously we would start watching for Mom's signal that enough time had passed. Once the okay was given, Jack and I would quickly retrieve the freezer, unwrap it and carefully lift out the can of frozen ice cream.

Large bowls would be scooped full for each of us to enjoy. Somehow, the icy mixture never lasted as long as we had anticipated. I don't know if that ice cream was really better, or if the effort and tiredness added a difference. But the ice cream of those summer days had a savory flavor that stands out in my boyhood memories and hasn't been matched yet.

What happened first in the story? Finish each sentence by making an X in the blank before the words that tell what happened.

1. Jack and his brother rode to the grocery store
   _____ when they had finished making ice cream.
   _____ to get ice to put in the ice cream freezer.
   _____ after they were tired of turning the freezer crank.
   _____ to escape summer chores.
2. The ice cream mixture was
   _____ poured directly into the crushed ice.
   _____ added to the can after the dasher was put in place.
   _____ added to the can before the dasher was put in place.
   _____ mixed in the kitchen by Dad.
3. The boy's arms ached because
   _____ turning the freezer crank was a hard job.
   _____ the ice was heavy to carry.
   _____ mixing the cream, eggs, and sugar took a lot of stirring.
   _____ the ice cream was hard to eat.
4. Which is the correct order of events in the story?
   _____ Mother suggested making ice cream, had Dad turn the crank,
   and invited the boys to share the ice cream.
   _____ The boys purchased ice at the store for Dad and Mother, and
   made ice cream alone.
   _____ Mom or Dad suggested making ice cream, the boys did their
   part of the cranking, and ice cream was served to everyone
   after it had ripened.
   _____ The boys mixed the ice cream, Dad turned the crank on the
   freezer, and Mom served ice cream to everyone.

Procedure:

1. Introduce written material to students by explaining that many
   things happen in specific order and that keeping events in order
   helps to make reading more interesting and informative as well
   as making the material much easier to understand.
2. Ask students to read the selection, trying to keep in mind the
   order of events in the material.
3. After reading the material, ask students to read the multiple
   choice questions and choose the correct answer for each.

Evaluation: Check answers of multiple choice questions and discuss.

Extended activities:

1. Have students write a story about an event that happened to the class. Are all stories the same? Did all report the event in the same order?
2. List the types of activities where it is important to have correctly ordered relationship, e.g., directions to follow, historical events, newspaper accounts.

STORY SETTING

Objective: The student will identify the setting of a story by naming the setting and identifying the clues that pertain to the setting.

Materials: prepared paragraphs (given below) written either on board or on dittoed sheets

Procedure:

1. Introduce concept by asking students, "Where are you now?"
2. Discuss with students the types of clues they would use to identify their location precisely.
3. Point out to students that writers use this same method to let the reader know where the story is taking place.
4. Have the students read the paragraphs and answer the questions that follow the readings.

WORKSHEET

Bennie was a happy mountain boy. He loved to roam over the shady paths of the rolling hills of North Carolina. He knew each and every pool of water where the large mountain bass waited to tease the eager fisherman. Often he tried his skill at landing those elusive creatures.

Nothing delighted Bennie more than a chance encounter with those gentle creatures, the deer. Silently he would stop suddenly and gaze at the immobilized statues until the deer, detecting the scent of a stranger, would gracefully run and leap off into the shelter of the woods.

1. Where did Bennie live? (North Carolina)
2. Name the clues that tell you where this is taking place. (mountain, rolling hills of North Carolina)

Angie sat on the steps and watched the house across the street with interest. As long she could remember, the "old Graham house," as everyone called it, had been empty. Long considered an eyesore by all the neighbors on Mulberry Street, it had been a pleasant surprise when workmen began to renovate the house two months ago. Diligent work had changed the neighborhood eyesore into the neighborhood showplace.

"I wonder what the new people will be like," Angie wondered as she watched the large moving van being unloaded. So far only a tall dark-haired man with a clipboard in his hand and two men wearing uniforms of the moving company had been seen. "I hope there are some children my age. It would be so nice to have friends right across the street. We would do all sorts of exciting things together. Guess I'll just have to wait and see," sighed Angie as she settled back more comfortably to watch the house across the street.

1. Where is Angie? (on Mulberry Street)
2. Name the clues that tell you where Angie is. (across the street, neighbors on Mulberry Street)

Al gazed intently out the window. Only one more hour and he would be free of the confining classroom and Mrs. Dexter's assignments. It wasn't that he minded the work or learning about history, but so many exciting things were happening in Middleton and he wanted to watch it happen. Thoughtfully he made his plans. First, I'll check the breeding ponds they're building at the edge of town. Maybe they are ready to stock the ponds with fish and begin operating the hatchery. After that I'll ride out and see how much more of the Interstate exchange is finished. Then if I have enough time. . .

"Al, would you please tell me. . ." Mrs. Dexter's voice pulled Al back to the realities of history class.

    1. Where is Al? (in history class)
    2. Name the clues that tell you where Al is. (classroom, learning about history)

Evaluation: Check students' oral or written answers to the questions.

Extended activity:

Have students compile a list of fictional characters and the setting of the stories.

RECALLING DETAILS (*How* Words)

Objective: Given written material, students will demonstrate ability in finding stated detail—*how* words.

Materials: worksheet for Follow-Up Activity #2

Procedure:

1. Write sentences on the chalkboard, omitting the word or words describing how the action occurred.

    Tom ran _____.
    Beth sang _____.
    The dog barked _____.

2. Have pupils suggest responses to complete each sentence. Explain that the word or words omitted are words that tell *how* the action occurred.
3. Write all pupil responses after the sentence.
4. Read each sentence, using the pupils' responses, or have an individual pupil read a sentence, supplying his or her response.
5. Discuss how each response tells *how* the action occurred. Explain that many *how* words end with -*ly*.

Extended activities:

1. Have pupils find and write all the words in a story read in their reader or a library book that tell how the action occurred.
2. Have prepared worksheets of sentences. Pupils underline the word or words in each sentence that tell how the action occurred.

    Tom ran *swiftly*.

3. Read sentences orally, having students identify the word or words telling *how* the action occurred.

RECALLING DETAILS (*Why* Words)

Objective: Given written material, students will demonstrate ability in finding stated details—*why* words.

Materials: worksheet for Follow-Up Activity #2

Procedure:

1. Write sentences on chalkboard, omitting the word or words telling why the action occurred:

    Mother baked a cake _____.
    David got the bat _____.
    Jim ran fast _____.

2. Have pupils supply words that would complete each sentence. Tell pupils that the part of the sentences omitted tells *why* the action occurred. Write suggested answers on the chalkboard after each sentence.
3. Read each sentence, supplying each of the suggested answers, or have a pupil read the sentence using his suggested part.
4. Lead pupils to discover that all the answers were words that tell *why* the action happened.

Extended activities:

1. Have pupils find and write words that tell *why* an action happened in a story read in their reader or a library book.

2. Have a prepared worksheet of sentences on which pupils are to underline the part of the sentence that tells why the action took place:

> Joe ran fast *to win the race*.

3. Read sentences orally, having pupils identify the words telling *why* the action occurred.

RECALLING DETAILS (*Where* Words)

Objective: Student will develop an awareness of words that tell *where* the action occurred or where the subject is located.

Materials: none for lesson; worksheet as described in Follow-Up Activity #2

Procedure:

1. Write sentences on the chalkboard, omitting the word or words telling where the action occurred:

> Mary sat _____.
> The coat was hanging _____.
> The dog hid his bone _____.

2. Have pupils supply a word or words to complete each sentence. Write each response after the sentence that tells where the action occurred.
3. Read each sentence and response or have pupils read the sentence and their response.
4. Discuss the fact that these words explained where the action took place.
5. Write other sentences, omitting the words that tell where the subject is located:

> The book _____ is Bill's.
> The dress _____ is new.
> The dog _____ is mine.

6. Repeat steps 2 and 3, using new responses.
7. Discuss the fact that words can also tell where the subject is.

Extended activities:

1. Have pupils find and write words that tell where the action occurred or where the subject is located in a story they have read or in library books.
2. Have a prepared worksheet with sentences using *where* words. Pupils underline the words that tell where the action occurred or the subject is located:

> The ball *under the tree* is mine.
> The hat was found *on the playground*.

RECALLING DETAILS (*When* Words)

Objective: Given written material, students will demonstrate ability in finding stated details—*when* words.

Materials: worksheet for Follow-Up Activity #2

Procedure:

1. Write sentences on the chalkboard, omitting word or words that tell when:

> I had a party ——.
> Mother took me to a movie ——.
> —— it will be cold.

2. Have pupils suggest responses for each sentence. Explain that the omitted word or words tell when. Write each pupil's response after the sentence.
3. Read all sentences using each response or have pupils read sentence using their response.
4. Discuss the fact that all the words used were words that told when the action happened.

Extended activities:

1. Have pupils find and write all the words that tell *when* on a certain page or pages in their readers or library books.
2. Have a worksheet of sentences. Pupils are to underline in each sentence the word or words that tell when the action happened:

> I went to the movie *last night*.
> *Tomorrow* I can go swimming.

3. Read sentences orally, having students identify the words that tell when the action occurred.

RECALLING DETAILS (*Who/What* Words)

Objective: Given written material, students will demonstrate ability in finding stated details—*who/what* words.

Materials: worksheet for Follow-Up Activity #2

Procedure:

1. Write sentences on the chalkboard, omitting the word stating who performed the action:

> _____ ran to the tree.
> _____ closed the door.
> _____ baked a cake.

2. Have pupils suggest words that could complete the sentence. Write each suggestion after the sentence.
3. Read each sentence using each suggestion, or let a pupil read the sentence using his word.
4. Lead pupils to discover that the word telling *who* or *what* did the action usually comes before the action word in a sentence.

Extended activities:

1. Have pupils find and write all the *who* and *what* words that appear on a certain page or pages in their reader or library book.
2. Have a prepared worksheet of simple sentences. Pupils are to

underline the word in each sentence that tells *who* or *what* performed the action:

> Tom ran very fast.
> The dog hid his bone.

RECALLING DETAILS (Action Words)

Objective: Given written material, students will demonstrate ability in finding stated details—*action* words.

Materials: worksheet for Follow-Up Activity #3

Procedure:

1. Write sentences on the chalkboard, omitting the action word:

> Bob _____ his bike.
> Jane _____ her new dress.

2. Have pupils supply any word or words they can think of to complete the sentence. Write all the responses after each sentence. Tell pupils the word missing is a word that tells the action or what the subject is doing.
3. Read each sentence with each response or let pupils read their response in the sentence.
4. Lead pupils to see that usually the action word comes right after the word that tells who or what did the action.

Extended activities:

1. Have pupils find and write the action words on a certain page or pages of a story or library book they have read.
2. Read sentences orally and have pupils act out the action word.
3. Have a worksheet of sentences. Pupils underline all the action words. Pupils can illustrate the action word.

Bill <u>ran</u> fast.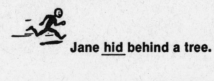

Jane <u>hid</u> behind a tree.

Brief Review–Literal and Comprehension Skills

Your students should now have developed ability in reading for understanding at the literal level. In case some need additional study or occasional review of these skills, we suggest you have them read whatever material you have available—library books, magazines, basals—as long as it is commensurate with their reading abilities. After a group has read the material, ask questions similar to the ones on these plans. Students will then apply these skills in a meaningful setting and at the same time receive review.

Establishment of literal comprehension ability is the criterion for moving your students onward to the more difficult reading skills, classified as interpretive and critical. These challenges await you in Chapters 7 and 8.

7

How to Improve
Interpretive Comprehension
Skills

If ever there were reading skills neglected by teachers, the cluster of interpretive comprehension skills beginning with Character Feelings (page 171) and continuing through Time Period (page 186) is likely to be that group. Wait! No aspersion is being cast at teachers, for they are generally given reading programs to follow and programs usually have shortcomings when it comes to helping teachers develop these skills. But now, with GALAXY'S Chapter 7, there is no need for your students to go without interpretive reading skill development.

Integrating these lessons with the reading program you are using is easy. First, follow the teacher's manual instructions, using professional discretion as you do. The reading selection and accompanying manual suggestions will revolve around one or more reading skills. The skill you think is most important is the one to emphasize after you have completed the activities from the manual. Teach the lesson or lessons (and extended activities) from this chapter which relate to the skill you are teaching. This procedure should nail down the skill for your students. Then continue with your reading program, again coming back to GALAXY for thorough treatment.

CAUSE AND EFFECT RELATIONSHIPS

Objective: Students will demonstrate ability to perceive cause and effect relationships.

Materials: none for lesson; worksheet for Follow-Up Activities #1 and #2

Procedure:

1. Write a topic sentence on the chalkboard:

   The boys and girls couldn't go skating.

2. Have pupils state reasons why the boys and girls couldn't go skating. List pupil responses under topic sentence (it rained, parents wouldn't let them, etc.).
3. Lead pupils to see that their answers were all causes, and the effect of those causes was the inability of the boys and girls to go skating.
4. Repeat steps 1-3 as often as necessary for understanding. Use different effect statements each time.
5. Write a topic sentence using a cause:

   Joe ate too much.

6. Have pupils relate effect statements, such as *so he got fat*.
7. Write responses on chalkboard under topic sentence.
8. Lead pupils to see that their effect statements resulted in the cause. Eating too much resulted or caused Joe to get fat, etc.
9. Discuss with pupils the fact that effects are the results of causes. Use as many examples as necessary.

Extended activities:

1. Have worksheet with cause/effect statements. Underline one part of the statement. Pupils identify if the underlined part is a cause or effect and identify it:

   We didn't have bread because there was no flour. (c)

   I didn't finish my homework so I couldn't watch T.V. (e)

2. Have worksheets. Pupils underline all causes and circle all effects:

   (I was sick) after I ate too many green apples.

3. Perform certain tasks, such as striking a match, turning on or off a light switch, getting a drink of water. Discuss with the students the action that represents the cause and the effect, such as: "What happened when the match was struck?"

PERCEPTION OF INFERENCE

Objective: Given reading material, students will demonstrate ability to formulate correct inferences by identifying the correct inference.

Materials: given below

Procedure:

1. Have the first paragraph of the following worksheet prepared either on the transparency or on the blackboard. The two sentences that follow the paragraph need to be covered so that they can not be read by the students.
2. Have the students read the paragraph. Then ask the students a couple of questions that require answers of specific information from the paragraph.
3. After the questions, stress to the students that they have used concrete information to answer, but that sometimes the material doesn't always give you a specific answer, in which case you must conclude or decide by information that is known.
4. Show the students the two covered sentences and ask, "Which statement do you think would apply to the paragraph we just read?"
5. Continue discussion as long as necessary with students until they understand that they are using facts to infer, or that they are deciding by using known facts.

6. Have the remaining paragraphs prepared either on other transparencies or on dittos. Have the students either work orally as above, or if dittos are used, independently, and then check.

WORKSHEET

Astronomy is the scientific study of the sun, moon, stars, and planets. The earth, which is also a planet, is part of that study. Astronomers, the scientists who study the heavenly bodies, help us to understand why the sun rises and sets and how the stars move in the sky. Knowing what the stars are made of and how stars create their light helps us to understand more about the heavenly system of which our planet is a part.

Astronomy is a science that is of little interest to only a few persons because of the specialized information.

Astronomy is a science that is of interest to many people because knowledge about it aids us in knowing more about our world.

Ancient people were also sky watchers. The sun which gave them heat and light was important to their life. These early astronomers measured time according to the position of the sun and the shape of the moon. Early man watched the sky for signs of the changing seasons so that he would know when to plant the crops needed for his family.

Astronomy is an old science which has been useful to man.

Astronomy is an old science which is of little use to man.

The Greeks were astronomers hundreds of years before the birth of Christ. They recorded the positions of the stars, the sun, and the moon so completely that eclipses of the sun and moon could be predicted. Ptolemy, a Greek who lived in Egypt about 150 A.D., published a book with the theory, or idea, that the earth was the center of the universe and that all heavenly bodies moved around it. This theory was so accepted by Greek and Arab astronomers that eventually European scholars learned of it also. For more than a thousand years, scholars of astronomy accepted and believed Ptolemy's idea of an earth-centered universe.

Scientific study of early astronomers was poorly done and scholars had little belief in one another's work.

Scientific study of early astronomy was exact work done by scholars who were often aware of work done by others in their field.

Evaluation: Check students as they work or check the completed dittoed sheets.

DRAWING CONCLUSIONS

Objective: The student will identify clues that lead to conclusions.

Materials: —books
—newspapers
—comic strips
—ditto sheet

Procedure:

1. Discuss words that refer to a place in time, but do not always refer to a date. Ask students if they know any words in this category. Some are: before, during, after, until, meantime, long ago, etc. Illustrate how sentences can have different meanings by writing on the board these sentences:

   Children did not go to school.
   Long ago, children did not go to school.

2. Conclusions can be brought about by facts the writer uses in his story or article. Newspapers are useful to illustrate this concept. Read an article to the class that tells the facts explicitly. Ask the class what conclusions they have formed. Discuss the difference between fact and fiction.

Fact: The house caught on fire and burned down.
Fiction: I think it was caused by some small child playing with matches. (opinion)

Words used in statements that are not represented as facts are maybe, perhaps, (I, we) think, might be.

3. Have students read a newspaper, choosing articles that state the author's conclusions. See if anyone can find an article that requires the reader to make his own conclusion. (Editorials are a good source.)

4. Discuss that students should be thinking as they read. Read a short story from the reading book and ask the students what questions they would ask themselves while reading it.

   Ask a question; see if it is supported in a paragraph.

5. Discuss the three main points in drawing a conclusion.

   1. Is it supported by facts?
   2. Is the conclusion based on opinion?
   3. Is the conclusion justified?

Illustrate the last point—*justified*. In order for a conclusion to be justified it must have the sentences or words to support it. Opinions can be used to justify a conclusion when evidence is given to support it.

   The earth's core is composed of molten rock. We have studied the mountains and oceans and our findings confirm this.
   (No one has ever been to the center of the earth, but the conclusion is justifiable because of the tests the author tells us about.)

Evaluation: Have students complete the following ditto assignment:

FACT OR OPINION? Write after each statement whether it is fact or opinion.

1. I believe that school is a good place to make friends. _____
2. It is a sunny day today and the weather report says that it will be the same tomorrow. _____
3. Perhaps if we all remain quiet, we will hear the birds sing. _____.

4. Students who do not hand in their homework are always lazy. _____.
5. Judy thinks that she is the smartest girl in the entire class. _____.

PREDICTION OF FUTURE ACTION BY DRAWING INFERENCES

Objective: Given stories to read, students will draw logical inferences from the reading material.

Procedure:

1. Give the students the definition of inference and have a brief discussion. (Making an inference implies arriving at a conclusion by reasoning from evidence.)
2. Give each student a skill worksheet. (See example on page 166.) After all have read the story, discuss the questions and the inferences derived from reading the story.
3. Display book jackets on a bulletin board. Have the children each pick a book jacket and write a story about what they think the book is about from looking at the jacket.

Evaluation: Observation during class discussion. Correctness of inferences made from reading skill booklet and from children's stories.

Extended activity:

If some children had difficulty grasping this concept, form a small group where you can work on a closer basis reinforcing with more stories and simple sentences from which students can make inferences.

MAIN IDEA (Titles)

Objective: Shown a picture and multiple titles, students will demonstrate their ability to know main ideas by selecting the best titles or stated actions.

WORKSHEET

Once there was a big brown bear who lived with his wife inside a cave.

"Please, dear," she said to him one day, "run down to the brook and catch some fish for dinner. But don't go near the beehive in the old dead tree. Remember what they did to you the last time."

Meanwhile the big brown bear walked slowly down the path toward the brook.

Of course, he had no intention of even looking at that beehive.

But, before he knew it, there he was heading straight for the old dead tree! He sniffed the good smell of honey and it made him walk faster, and the faster he walked, the better it smelled.

............?............

Do you think the big brown bear continued to the beehive? What do you think the bear did when he reached the beehive? Why do you think so? What do you think was the reaction of the bees? Why do you think so?

PREDICTION OF FUTURE ACTION BY DRAWING INFERENCES

What Friend Am I?

Soft and furry am I.
I have hair all over.
I think you like to play with me.
Around my neck is a pink ribbon.
Children like to hold me and I like that!
Sometimes you take me to bed with you.

............?............

We are outside.

It is raining.

We do not have an umbrella.

?

Materials: five pictures appropriate for giving a title

Procedure:

1. Show pupils one of the five pictures. Talk about what is happening in the picture. Give pupils three choices of titles (orally) and have them choose the title that would best go with the picture.

A Good Day for Fishing

A Summer Day

A Big Pond

2. Repeat step 1, using two more of the pictures.
3. For the last two pictures, discuss each, then have pupils offer suggestions for a title. Write each suggestion on the chalkboard. Discuss each suggested title.
4. Write on the chalkboard or have prepared worksheet words that would describe an action. Have three choices of titles. Read the words, then the titles. Have pupils choose the best title.

   A) train-tracks-fast-new-places-slow-stop
   B) airplane-loud noise-high-fast-low-land

   A) School Days
      A Day at the Circus
      A Train Ride

   B) A Long Jump
      A Huge Fire
      An Airplane Ride

5. Discuss how titles tell the main idea.

Extended activities:

1. Use comic strips and write a title for the strip.
2. Have pictures. List words that describe the picture. Make up a title.

MAIN IDEA (Details)

Objective: Given details, students will demonstrate ability for getting the main idea.

Materials: comic strip for #3 Follow-Up Activity

Procedure:

1. Write four titles and many descriptive phrases on the chalkboard:

   1. A Boat Trip
   2. First Day at School
   3. The Library
   4. A Bad Dream

   (3) books on a shelf
   (2) seeing new friends
   (3) people selecting books

   (4) monsters after you
   (1) going to lake
   (2) eating in the cafeteria
   (2) meeting a new teacher

   (1) taking a fishing pole
   (4) seeing scary things
   (3) a lady putting books on shelves
   (1) starting the motor
   (4) waking up afraid
   (1) wearing a bathing suit
   (2) working math problems

2. Talk about each phrase.
3. Have pupils decide which title the phrase is describing.
4. Have pupils write the number of the title by the phrase, as shown in the example in step 1.
5. Discuss with pupils how finding sentence detail phrases or words can help when seeking the main idea.

Extended activities:

1. Write a sentence using familiar words and have pupils illustrate the sentence.
2. Have pupils match, check, or write words or phrases for a picture which is described:

       ___ a warm day
       ___ fun with water
       ___ rain and wind

3. Have pupils write descriptive words or phrases for a comic strip or picture.

FINDING THE MAIN IDEA (Paragraphs)

Objective: Students will locate main idea in differing parts of paragraphs.

Materials: none

Procedure:

1. Explain that the main idea or point of a paragraph can be found either at the first, middle, or end of a paragraph.
2. Explain that one sentence usually tells the main idea of the paragraph and the remaining sentences are supporting sentences that tell about the main idea.
3. Illustrate the main idea of a paragraph when the first sentence is the main idea by drawing a Δ on the chalkboard and reading a short paragraph, such as:

> Bob wanted a new baseball glove. The one he had was old. He started saving his money. Soon he had enough money to buy a new glove.

4. Discuss which sentence is the main idea and write that sentence

at the top of the triangle. List the supporting sentences at the base.

Bob wanted a new baseball glove.

The one he had was old.
He started saving his money.
Soon he had enough money to
buy a new glove.

5. Continue with other paragraphs. Give as much practice as needed.

> *Note:* Lesson in which the main idea is found in the middle or at the end of a paragraph can be developed using the same format, only using ▽ for main ideas stated in the last sentence and ⋈ for main ideas stated in the middle.

Tom was the top speller in
the contest.
Joe was second.
Mary was in third place.

There were three finalists
in the spelling contest.

The children walked to the
park.
They bought ice cream

They were finding
things to do.

They couldn't go to the movie
until three o'clock.
Time sure was moving slowly.

Extended activities:

1. Have sentences in a paragraph cut into strips, one sentence per strip. Have pupils find the sentence that is the main idea. Then have pupils arrange the sentences so that the main idea sentence is the first sentence, then the middle sentence, and finally the last sentence.
2. Have pupils find paragraphs in other books in which the main idea sentence is the first sentence, middle sentence, or last sentence.
3. Give students a short paragraph. Have them rewrite the paragraph, putting the main idea in another place. If the main idea is first, they are to put it in the middle or end.

CHARACTER FEELINGS

Objective: The student will demonstrate the ability to recognize character feelings by choosing the correct response to questions about character feelings.

Materials: given below

Procedure:

1. Ask students, "How do you know how someone is feeling?"
2. What are the different ways people feel? (Good, confident, sad, discouraged, etc.)
3. Use their responses to lead students to the fact that sometimes we use what people say to determine how they feel. Point out to students that authors often use the words of a character to tell how they feel.
4. Have students read through the diary given below. Ask them to see if they can tell how the young man feels about his experience.

WORKSHEET

These paragraphs are from the diary of a young settler whose family is going to California. How does he feel about his family's traveling?

29 March:

At last. After spending the long winter months here in St. Joe, spring is here and Captain Pentleton says that he is ready to start for the West. We have waited so long for those words. Once again we checked our supplies for they must last the many months it takes us to cross the prairies and desert on our way to California territory. We have corn meal, flour, sugar, dried beans, coffee, bacon, and some apples Mother dried last fall after we got to St. Joe. We also have the tools we need to repair our wagon and to clear land once we find a homestead. Everything we have in the world is packed into the wagon. Tomorrow we're on our way!

14 May:

It has rained and rained and rained. Everything we have is wet. Water drips from the canvas wagon top and nothing is dry. We can't even light a fire because there is nothing to burn and even if there was, the rain has come down steady for two days now. All we had to eat was cold beans and the corn pone Ma fixed Wednesday just before the rain started. I'm wet and cold. I wish we were back home!

29 July:

We've been traveling for so many weeks now that I can hardly remember anything but the bouncing of the wagon. I'm so tired of the endless ride. At first, traveling was pleasant. But now that we've left the green hills and trees all we can see is the endless brown of the prairie. We haven't seen a real tree in days, only those little clumps of bushes that hug the small creeks that aren't completely dry yet. And the sun, it beats down day after day and there's not a bit of shade except for the canvas Dad tied over the seat of the wagon. Won't this journey ever end?

November 4:

It's been a long hard trip but we made it. We've climbed mountains, forded creeks and rivers, and traveled in all kinds of weather. We traveled on the best of days and the worst of days. It was a rugged journey and we worked hard to make it. Now, we can do whatever is necessary to get settled in this bright new land of California.

QUESTIONS

1. In the first paragraph, the young man
   1. is ready to begin the trip west.
   2. does not want to leave St. Joe.
   3. needs more time to get supplies for the trip.

2. In the second paragraph, the young man
   1. is looking forward to the rest of the journey.
   2. is discouraged by all the rain.
   3. is planning to go back home.

3. In the third paragraph, the young man
   1. is enjoying the trip.
   2. feels like he is on an endless journey.
   3. is enjoying the fresh air and sunshine.

4. In the last paragraph, the young man
   1. is satisfied to have finished his trip.
   2. is satisfied that the trip is finished and is confident about the future.
   3. is unhappy that the trip was so long.

Evaluation: Completed worksheet. Discuss and check answers together.

CHARACTER ANALYSIS RELATED TO CHARACTER ACTIONS

Objective: The student will use character analysis to describe or justify character actions.

Materials: given below

Procedure:

1. Ask students how they can tell how someone feels; look for response that says by watching how a person acts.

2. List some actions that would indicate how a person feels—happy when praised by someone, mad when scolded, etc.
3. Have students read written material and work accompanying exercises.

WORKSHEET

All day long Karen had waited for her birthday present, but neither Mom nor Dad had even so much as mentioned that today was her birthday. Somehow, something was wrong and Karen was getting very worried.

"Karen, will you come here?" Mrs. French called to Karen from the hallway.

Slowly Karen got to her feet and walked to the doorway. "Here I am, Mom," she started to say as she walked into the hall.

"Happy birthday, dear," said Mr. and Mrs. French.

All Karen could do was smile widely and nod her head because in front of her parents stood the very bike she had hoped to get for her birthday. Bright blue paint covered the bike while ribbons of red, white, and blue topped off the shiny handle bars. It was complete, even to the white wicker basket hanging over the front bar.

"It's beautiful," sighed Karen as she rushed to hug her parents, "It's beautiful. Oh, thank you."

At first, Karen was (a) worried, (b) sad, (c) unconcerned that her parents had forgotten her birthday.

When she saw the bike, Karen was (a) angry because her parents had picked the wrong present, (b) glad they had gotten exactly what she wanted, (c) wished her parents had gotten something else.

Tim had worked on the model rocket for weeks. Carefully he had glued the pieces together and then painted the body and trim. Now at last he had a real replica of the rocket the astronauts would use for the Sky Lab mission. Smiling, he took one more look at his rocket and then left for school.

That afternoon when he came home, Tim was startled to find his rocket lying on the floor in pieces and beside it the kickball of his brother Mike.

"Tim, I—" Mike said as he started to come in Tim's room.

"What did you do?" demanded Tim. "I'm telling Mom. You aren't supposed to be in my room when I'm at school."

"Tim, it was an accident. I didn't mean to break it."

"That's what you always say. You better get out of here and take that dumb ball too. Go on, get out of here," replied Tim.

Tim was (a) pleased and happy, (b) unhappy and displeased, (c) unconcerned about the model being built.

When Tim found the broken rocket he was (a) unhappy, (b) glad, (c) mad.

Tim was (a) willing, (b) unwilling to listen to Mike's explanation.

Patty had done everything exactly as Mrs. Howard had shown them how in Home Ec class. Carefully she had planned the menu and shopped for the groceries. All afternoon she had worked preparing the food and setting the table. Everyone was going to be so surprised.

"Hi, dear, hmm, something smells good!" Mrs. Jerkins said as she came in the door.

"Mom, I fixed dinner. Everything is ready; want to see?" offered Patty.

"Oh, did you, dear? That's too bad," answered Mrs. Jerkins.

"What do you mean?" asked Patty.

"Well, Daddy called before I left the office and he and I are going out to dinner with a client of his. We've already said that we'd go. You and Dale will be the only ones here for dinner."

"June, how long before you're ready to go?" the voice of Mr. Jerkins could be heard from the garage.

"Oh, Mom, I worked so hard. Can't you go out another night?" wailed Patty as tears welled in her eyes.

"There, there, dear," consoled Mrs. Jerkins. "Everything looks lovely and it smells delightful. I'm sorry that you went to so much trouble. We'll make it up somehow."

Patty was (a) confident that she had planned a nice surprise,

(b) unsure that she had planned a nice dinner, (c) worried that her mother would fix dinner.

Patty was (a) happy her parents were going out, (b) unhappy her parents were going out, (c) happy she was going out.

Patty was (a) delighted, (b) depressed, (c) disappointed because her surprise was spoiled.

Evaluation: Check worksheets and discuss with students.

Extended activity:

Prepare cards (any size) on which an emotion or feeling is written and place them in a box. Have a student select a card and act out the emotion or feeling. The other students then try to guess the word being acted. This may be played in teams or small groups. Students may add other words to the word box if desired.

Suggested words: happy, sad, frightened, pleased, angry, euphoric, elated, grieved, confident, unsure, peeved, impatient, sullen, joyful, cheerful.

PERCEPTION OF SENSORY IMAGERY

Objective: The students will demonstrate perception of sensory imagery by selecting and describing the most intense or appropriate imagery for a given sense.

Materials: ditto of poems given below and a ditto of sentences for evaluation

Procedure:

1. Read the poem "Mud."

Mud

Mud is very nice to feel
All squishy-squash between the toes!
I'd rather wade in wiggly mud
Than smell a yellow rose.

Nobody else but the rosebud knows
How nice mud feels
Between the toes.

2. Discuss which sense was appealed to and why.
3. Read the poem "First Snow."

First Snow

Snow makes whiteness where it falls,
The bushes look like popcorn balls.
And places where I always play,
Look like somewhere else today.

4. Discuss which sense was appealed to and why.
5. Read the poem "Junior."

Junior

My Daddy smells like tobacco and books,
Mother like lavender and Listerine;
Uncle John carries a whiff of cigars,
Nannie smells starchy and soapy and clean.

6. Again discuss the sensuous elements of the poem.
7. Read "Aeroplane."

Aeroplane

There's a humming in the sky
There's a shining in the sky
Silver wings are flashing by
Silver wings are shining by
Aeroplane
Aeroplane
Flying-high

Silver wings are shining
As it goes gliding by
First it zooms
And it booms
Then it buzzes in the sky

Then its song is just a drumming
A soft little humming
Strumming
Strumming

8. Discuss "Aeroplane."

9. Read "Lemons."

Lemons

A lemon's a lemony kind of thing
It doesn't look sharp and it doesn't look sting
It looks rather round and it looks rather square
It looks almost oval; a yellowy pear.
It looks like a waxy old, yellow old pear,
It looks like a pear without any stem,
It doesn't look sharp and it doesn't look sting.
A lemon's a lemony kind of a thing,
But cut it and touch it with tongue
You'll see where the sharp and the sting
    have been hiding—
Under the yellow without any warning
I touch and touch it again with my tongue
I like it! I like it! I like to be stung!

10. Discuss the sensory images conveyed in "Lemons."

Evaluation:

1. Give a list of several sentences that appeal to different senses of
   the students and have them label each sentence with the sense to
   which it appeals.

   1. The tick of the clock seemed to grow louder and louder.
      (hearing)
   2. The kitten's ear was soft like velvet. (touch)
   3. The sweet juice of the watermelon pleased him. (taste)
   4. The white marble building was shining in the sun. (sight)
   5. The air was fresh with the odor of newly cut grass. (smell)
   6. David thought the television program was very interesting (sight;
      hearing)
   7. The steaks were tender and juicy. (taste; touch)

    8. The siren shrieked throughout the town. (hearing)
    9. Skins of peaches are fuzzy and hairy. (touch)
  10. The aroma of bread was in the air. (smell)

2. Ask the students to select poems that appeal to each of the five senses. They must tell why and how.

Extended activity:

Have the students write poems that appeal to the senses.

RECOGNITION AND EMPLOYMENT OF IDIOMS AND FIGURATIVE LANGUAGE

Materials: none

Procedure:

1. Write the following sentence on the board:

   When he awoke the morning after his tennis game, Ted was stiff as a board.

2. Ask students if Ted was really so stiff that he looked like a board.
3. Discuss with students what the sentence means.
4. Explain that when we use an expression to represent an idea in a sentence without taking the words literally, we are employing *figurative* language.
5. Explain to students that when we say that Ted was stiff as a board, we are using a simile to describe how Ted felt, to get the idea across that he was very stiff from his strenuous exercise.
6. Ask students to think of other similes that relate to the way they are feeling today, or recent experiences, or just expressions they have heard that may be called similes.
7. Write the sentence, "He had a heart of gold," on the board.
8. Ask students if his heart was really made out of gold.
9. Explain that when we have an expression that implies a comparison but omits the words "as" or "like," that expression is called a metaphor.

10. Write the sentence, "The boy was as tall as the Jolly Green Giant," on the board.
11. Ask students if they believe that the boy in this sentence was as tall as the Jolly Green Giant.
12. After discussion, explain that a figure of speech that uses exaggeration for emphasis is called *hyperbole*.
13. Ask students to think of examples of hyperbole.
14. Write the sentence, "Duty calls," on the board. Explain that this sentence is an example of a figure of speech called personification. Explain that personification means endowing animals, plants and inanimate objects or concepts with personal traits or human attributes or capabilities.
15. Ask students to think of examples of personification.
16. Write the following words on the board:

   Personification—
   Hyperbole—
   Metaphor—
   Simile—

17. Ask students to define each figure of speech and give an example of each. Write definitions and examples on the board next to the words.

FIGURATIVE EXPRESSIONS

Objective: Given a set of sentences containing figurative expressions, the student will identify figurative speech as an element of style by written explanation of the speech.

Materials: list of figurative speech expressions

Procedure: There are four types of figurative speech:

   a. Placing of opposite ideas side by side—"That is the long and short of it."
   b. Exaggerating—"He jumped a mile high."

    c. Comparing one thing with another—"He lives like a king."
    d. Giving human qualities to something non-human—"The wind screamed."

1. Use examples to explain to students that figurative speech is a means by which the author shows a more vivid picture or suggests a relationship to the reader.
2. Discuss the examples and have students make up their own expressions of figurative speech.

WORKSHEET

John is *a hot-head*.
_____

We were *as snug as a bug in a rug.*
_____

He ran *like lightning.*
_____

Helen's eyes *swept* the shore.
_____

Evaluation: Give students a prepared sheet with several figurative expressions. They are to write the literal meaning of each expression.

Extending Activity:

    Construct a gameboard and a set of figurative expression cards and a set of literal meaning statement cards. As students move around the board, they are to match the figurative expression with the literal meaning. Game may be played by two, three or four players.

SIMILES AND METAPHORS

Objective: Students will recognize and identify similes and metaphors in reading matter and oral material.

Materials: worksheets

Procedure: Begin by teaching what similes are, as in the lesson that follows.

1. A simile is a comparison between two unlike things that are similar in at least one respect.

   Notice the words *simile* and *similar*.

   In stating the comparison, the words "like" or "as" are used.

   A simile uses one object to help describe another. This creates a vivid picture that appeals to our senses.

   > "Your eyes are as bright as the stars."
   > (Your eyes and the stars are similar because they both are bright.)
   >
   > "The children chattered like monkeys."
   > (The children and the monkeys are similar because both chattered.)

2. Similes enrich our language and make it possible to see things in a new way.

quick as a fox	thin as a rail
teeth like pearls	fat as a pig
red as a beet	soft as silk
hard as nails	quick as a wink

3. In learning to identify similes, we will scan sentences for the words "like" or "as." This may cause us to identify a statement incorrectly, such as "She is like her sister." We should try to state explicitly the comparison being made between two unlike things.

   > Your hands are *as cold as ice.*
   > Her dress is *as red as an apple.*
   > She is like her mother.
   > The clouds look *like fluffy cotton.*
   > As I walked home I watched the trees sway.
   > He is *as clever as a fox.*
   > He is *as strong as an ox.*
   > She is *as quiet as a mouse.*

4. When similes are overused they lose their appeal. Here are some common similes. Use your imagination to change the simile to make your own comparison.

quick as a fox	_____as a rail
teeth like pearls	quick as a _____
thin as a rail	teeth like _____
fat as a pig	_____ as a pig
	red as _____
	quick as _____
	soft as a _____

5. Have students complete the following worksheet.

WORKSHEET

Write as many similes as you can using the names of animals. For example: "You are as wise as an owl."

Write as many similes as possible to express the idea in this sentence: "He is tall."

Complete the following similes. Use your imagination!

_____ as a rail

quick as a _____

teeth like _____

_____ as a pig

red as _____

quick as _____

soft as _____

6. Teach what metaphors are.

A metaphor is an implied comparison without the words "like" or "as." When reading for metaphors, be sure to understand what is being compared and how they are similar.

"She has a voice of honey."
(Her voice and honey are similar because both are sweet and smooth.)

"His shirt is a rainbow of colors."
(His shirt and a rainbow are similar because both have many colors.)

In using metaphors, a vivid picture is created that gives the reader enjoyment. The five senses (sight, smell, taste, touch, and hearing) are often used in metaphors.

Her voice dripped with honey.
The lawn was a carpet.
A peaches and cream complexion.

Explain the metaphors used in these sentences:

I don't like to eat those rock cookies.
(Cookies can be hard as rocks.)

Her voice dripped honey as she talked.
(Her voice was sweet and smooth like honey.)

The ribbon of water flowed slowly through the plain.
(The water's path was narrow and winding like a ribbon.)

The foxy hunter was creeping through the woods.
(The hunter was clever and sly like a fox.)

7. Present the following worksheet.

WORKSHEET

Think of a similarity between pairs of words. Write metaphors expressing this similarity.

moonlight _____
_____

fingers _____
_____

carpet _____
_____

meadow _____
_____

man _____
_____

tiger _____
_____

snow _____

_____

ivory _____

_____

Write metaphors substituting one of the given words in each sentence:

The man is a skyscraper. _____

_____

His feet are balloons. _____

_____

He is a dime sideways. _____

_____

His voice is loud. _____

_____

PERCEPTION OF MOOD

Objective: Students will demonstrate ability to define and understand perception of mood in reading.

Materials: blackboard, chalk, eraser

Procedure:

1. Create mood by turning out the lights. Discuss with the students their changes of moods.
2. Define mood as the emotional coloring of a story, which the author tries to create by choice of words or images.
3. Discuss the importance of perceiving mood in a story: the fact that it is critical to story comprehension. Cite a few words such as "tears," "painful," "ecstatic," and "happy" to students, telling them that grasping the mood of a story is important in understanding and appreciating the story, and the key to the mood is emotion words or description of behavior—words such as those you have just mentioned.
4. Discuss the three main emotions—sadness, happiness, fear. For

concrete reinforcement, have students role-play the three emotional expressions.

5. On a higher level, have the students draw an example of a sad, happy, and fearful face on the board.
6. Write the three basic emotions on the blackboard and have the students give more examples of each, listing them in their proper categories.
7. Give the students a series of words and have them respond by naming the correct mood.
8. Read to the students short passages (literature books are great) and have them identify the mood.

Evaluation: Observation of students' work on the blackboard and participation in role-playing mood expressions.

Extended activities:

1. Have students define the mood created in a book or in a particular chapter.
2. Have students bring to class newspaper clippings representing different moods.
3. Have students watch their favorite TV programs and discuss in class the different moods portrayed.

TIME PERIOD

Objective: The student will demonstrate ability to recognize the time period of written material by using facts or clues given in the material.

Materials: dittoed worksheet (given on facing page)

Procedure:

1. Discuss with students the types of clues authors use to tell the reader the time of the activity.

2. Make a list of the types of clues used, such as types of clothing characters wear, types of items used or described, etc. List as many clues as possible.
3. Have students read and work ditto worksheets.

WORKSHEET

As the jets roared overhead, Mike shaded his eyes against the glare of the afternoon sun to get a better look at the silver streaks. Wish I were riding on that, Mike thought. I'll bet being a jet pilot is the most exciting job in the world. Imagine! Soaring above the clouds, skimming from city to city in hours. Suddenly a tap on Mike's shoulder brought Mike's attention abruptly back to earth.

"Hey, Mike, going to the game today?" demanded Steve. "What's the matter? That's the third time I've asked you."

"Oh, sorry Steve, guess my mind was on something else. I don't know, I have to check and see if Mr. Peters needs me at work first. If he does then I can't go, if he doesn't, well, I'm not sure. I'll let you know later, okay?"

The time of this conversation is

in the past
(x) in the present
in the future

What clue or clues help you to determine the time here? (Jets, which are common today.)

"Plum foolishness!"

"Never seen anything like that before," chimed another voice.

"Imagine, fifteen miles an hour! What won't they think of next!" The voice of Mr. Barker the grocer was easily identified above the crowd.

Jeremiah Browning inched his way forward into the crowd to see what everyone was talking about. Must be something special, he thought, to have everyone so stirred up. Then he saw it. A shiny red horseless carriage parked right on the town square.

"Oh," Jeremiah whispered in a long drawn out breath as he stretched his hand out hesitantly to touch the dirt-steaked side of the car.

"Careful, boy, that's a dangerous machine there," warned a deep voice.

Jeremiah jerked his hand back. "I wasn't going to hurt anything."

"I know, boy, It's hard enough for me to keep my hands off and I helped build it."

The time of this conversation is

(x) in the past
     in the present
     in the future

What clue or clues help you to determine the time here? (Speed of car—fifteen miles an hour; horseless carriage.)

Roy Dickerson settled back into the comfort of the lounge seat. "It's been a very impressive trip, Captain. You and your men are to be congratulated."

"Thank you, sir," replied Captain John Everly. "We've worked very hard to get everything ready for your inspection. You know, when my team and I arrived, this planet was absolutely bare. Now, look, we've got a landing facility set up for the trans-galaxy rockets, the machinery in place to do the actual mining of materials, and suitable housing complete with atmospherically correct quarters ready for the workers. Do you know when they'll be arriving?"

"The satelite report yesterday confirmed that the rockets had left Skylab on schedule last week. If all goes well, they should arrive from the Milky Way Galaxy in a month or so. In the meantime, Captain, if you and your men will just remain until they arrive, the Galaxy Commission would be most appreciative of your efforts.

"You can count on us, Mr. Dickerson," answered Captain Everly. "We of the Galaxatic Exploration and Settlement Force are always at your service."

The time of this conversation is

     in the past
     in the present
(x) in the future

What clue or clues help you to determine time here? (Trans-galaxy rockets, atmospherically correct cities, travel from Milky

Way Galaxy, Galaxatic Commission, Galaxatic Exploration and Settlement Force which do not exist now.)

Evaluation: Check students' worksheets, discussing with students the clues that helped them to make their choices.

Extended activity:

Make a chart of clues which may be used to show time.

	PRESENT	PAST	FUTURE
transportation	cars	carriages	electric cars
	motorcycles	covered wagons	space belts

Brief Review–Interpretive Comprehension Skills

Once you have taught these interpretive comprehension lessons you know you have made significant headway with your students, even though they have had varying degrees of success. Whatever the success level reached by each student, that person will need additional practice in using these high level reading skills in a variety of reading material. So we recommend that you follow up these lessons with many opportunities for your students to develop practice and extend their interpretive skills.

Use of small grouping arrangements in which discussion is carried on after everyone has read the same selection is one way to extend learnings. Another is to have individual reading passages available with questions to be answered. Students can read, answer the questions, and check their responses for correct answers if answer keys are available. All these things (reading passages, questions and answer keys) could be located on a table, a countertop, a spare desk or anywhere else you have an available spot. In this way, you can individualize your instruction, allowing for self-pacing and self-correction, while at the same time providing the necessary additional reading skill practice.

8
Teaching Critical Comprehension Skills

Few reading programs include the wide array of critical comprehension skills provided in this chapter. At your fingertips are lessons for recognizing fables, satire, myths, irony, fanciful language, understanding author's purpose, syntax, identification of persuasive techniques and others. You will be able to meet the critical reading skill needs of your students.

Multiple lesson plans are provided for two of the skills in this chapter. One of these is "Fact or Opinion" which has two lessons not only because this skill is important—as all of them are—but also because it is often included in literacy tests which are being employed in several states. Although we disclaim any implication that the teaching of fact and opinion identification can be done in two lessons, we think you can use these as models; and by substituting information, you could develop additional plans with little effort, tailoring them to your own students and locale.

Also, we have a two-lesson series for developing the understanding of symbolism. We think you should begin with the concrete notion that symbols represent ideas; thus the first lesson, "Symbols," is a good introduction because your students will learn to identify symbols. Building upon that, the other lesson, "Symbolism," will enable you to teach students recognition of the author's use of symbolism in passages. We think it is better to teach the easier lesson first because it is a foundation for the second.

With the building blocks in this chapter, you will have the framework for developing these difficult but critical reading skills. Remember that simple alterations and substitutions in these generic lesson plans can increase your teaching power. For example, after John Donne's "No Man Is an Island" is used another poem could be used for additional symbolic value. Such alterations and substitutions will increase your ability to make these skills well learned and of functional value to your readers.

ABILITY TO MAKE JUDGMENTS

Objective: The student will demonstrate the ability to make judgments by orally stating the proper answer to the questions asked by the teacher, by reading the questions provided in the worksheet and drawing a line around the one word that answers each question.

Materials: worksheet that provides practice in making judgments

Procedure:

1. Write on the board questions that have only one correct answer:

   Which goes faster—a car or a bicycle?
   Are children older or younger than adults?
   Do you have five or ten fingers on one hand?
   Are three girls and four boys six children or seven children?

2. Discuss with students the answers to these questions. Check to see if all students are participating and are correctly answering the questions. The questions you write on the board should vary in difficulty in relation to your grade level.

3. Ask students if they can think of any questions similar to the ones on the board so you can see that they understand.

4. Hand out worksheet. (See facing page.)

Evaluation: Check the worksheet. If some students have missed some answers discuss with them why they circled what they did. If necessary, prepare another worksheet.

WORKSHEET

DIRECTIONS: Read the question and draw a line around the one
word that answers each question.

1. Do you cross the street on the green light or red light?
2. If you weigh too much, are you overweight or underweight?
3. Upon seeing a funny incident, do you cry or laugh?
4. After dinner, are you hungry or full?
5. When a dog wags its tail, is it vicious or contented?
6. Which goes faster—a train or a ship?
7. Are adults older or younger than children?
8. If you broke a dish, would your mother be likely to smile or to
   grimace?
9. To develop friendships, should you be cool or nice to people?
10. Should helping other people make you feel happy or aloof?

Extended activities:

1. Prepare worksheets like the one used here.
2. Ask for questions that involve the students in making judgments.
3. Have students read the questions and write the answer they
   would use to answer the question.

RECOGNITION OF FABLES

Objective: The student is to identify a fable as a short story, usually
with animal characters displaying human qualities,
which teaches a lesson or value.

Materials: copies of *Aesop's Fables*

Procedure:

1. Read two or more fables to the students.
2. Explain that these stories were used as ways to teach people
   "morals" or ways of behaving without offending them.
3. Define "moral" as a lesson or value about behavior.
4. Have students identify the problem of each fable.
5. Have the students explain the values or morals being taught by
   the fable in their own words.

Evaluation:

1. Give the students a fable; they are to identify the problem of the fable and the moral being taught.
2. Have the student write a fable, using animals with human characteristics, which teaches a moral.

Extended activity:

1. Have students dramatize fables, using puppets.
2. Explore the fables of various other cultures.

RECOGNITION OF SATIRE

Objective: The student will demonstrate a recognition of satire as a literary form by identifying or describing it, or by identifying the techniques involved and their effect.

Materials: —political cartoons from magazines or newspaper glued on construction paper
—comic strips (many of which satirize situations which need to be improved)

Procedure:

1. Explain how satire is a technique that uses humor and wit to help one understand and laugh at one's own failings and foibles. Explain how it can range from gentle ridicule to bitter derision.
2. Show examples of cartoons; discuss how and why satire is being used.
3. Have students examine cartoons and comic strips. Have them identify the subject or person being satirized.
4. Have students use newspapers, magazines, or books to find examples of satire. They are to explain the characteristics that make each example satire.

Evaluation:

Give students several selections of reading, one of which is satire. Student is to identify the satire selection.

Extended activity:

1. Have students watch a comedy show and look for elements of satire. Discuss in class.
2. Have students draw own cartoons and use satire in picture or captions.

RECOGNITION OF MYTHS

Objective: The student will identify myths as traditional stories about supernatural beings or heros of a culture, and as the means by which life and natural phenomena are explained by a culture.

Materials: mythical stories from different cultures—Greek, Norse, American Indian

Procedure:

1. Ask students how they would explain a natural occurrence to a younger child. Discuss their response.
2. Read a myth about a natural phenomenon.
3. Discuss why stories were made up to explain things that people could not explain easily.
4. Have students read and compare myths of different cultures. Discuss similarities and differences.

Evaluation: Ask students to read several short selections. They are to identify the myth and explain what event or phenomenon it explains.

Extended activity:

1. Have student compare a myth and the scientific explanation of the same natural phenomenon.
2. Draw pictures of myths or a mural for the class. Write a modern day myth about something about which we have only theories, such as the origin of the solar system.

RECOGNITION OF IRONY

Objective: The student will identify the author technique of irony by defining it or its purpose or use in written material.

Materials: given below

Procedure:

1. Define *irony* as the use of a work, expression, or combination of words to produce a result the opposite of what may be expected.
2. Discuss examples of irony with students.

> The St. Bernard named Tiny. . .
> The van stolen from a police station. . .
> The doctor who faints while getting a shot. . .

3. Have the students rewrite sentences to produce an ironical effect:

> The florist loved working among the roses.
> The florist was allergic to the roses.
>
> Our dog, a German shepherd, barked whenever strangers knocked on the door.
> Our dog, a German shepherd, hid under the bed when anyone knocked on our door.
>
> The photographer snapped lovely pictures.
> The photographer snapped all the pictures with the lens cover on the camera.
>
> The radio was stolen.
> The radio was stolen from the police car.

Evaluation: Have the students work the following worksheet:

WORKSHEET

Sentences containing examples of author use of irony are to be marked by an "I" in the blank provided before the sentence.

___(I)___ 1. The fire station was set afire by the firemen.

_____ 2. The swimmer won three relay races and a diving contest.

__(I)__ 3. Duke, our watchdog, tucked his tail under and slunk away when Cathy's kitten hissed and spat at him.

_____ 4. The teenagers worked tirelessly to repair the children's playground.

__(I)__ 5. The swimmer, helped down from the high diving board because he was dizzy, was a pilot.

__(I)__ 6. The street was covered with pamphlets written by the Anti-Littering Campaign Committee.

_____ 7. Robin Hood robbed the rich and gave to the poor.

__(I)__ 8. Psychologists state that more people are unhappy at Christmas than at any other time of the year.

_____ 9. The winning basket was thrown just as the buzzer sounded to end the basketball game.

__(I)__10. Pete Roscoe, the leading hitter of the sandlot baseball team, broke his toe this afternoon when he hit it with a low bat swing.

Extended activities:

Have students use cartoons or everyday situations to create ironical situations.

RECOGNITION OF FANCIFUL LANGUAGE

Objectives: The student will identify the author technique of fanciful language by identifying its use and purpose in written material and by rewriting phrases or sentences in this technique.

Materials: given below

Procedure:

1. Define fanciful language to the students as an author technique used to embellish descriptions or paint more vivid images in the reader's mind.
2. Discuss the examples below, contrasting the author statements so that the use of fanciful language is clear to the students:

> The orchard was lit by moonlight.
> The orchard shimmered in silver moonrays.

The stars shone in the sky.
Twinkling diamonds sparkled against the blue velvet sky.

Bees hummed in the woods.
The whole woods resounded with a thousand voices of humming bees and droning wasps.

3. Have students rewrite some sentences, using the fanciful language technique:

The garden was pretty.
(Ex.-Multicolored hues of the flowers made the garden a pretty place.)

The brook ran over the hill.
(Ex.-The brook twisted and tumbled over the rocky hillside.)

Low branches of the tree touched the ground.
(Ex.-Great arms of the trees clung to the ground.)

Evaluation: Give the students the following list of sentences or similar examples. The student is to identify the sentences that contain author use of fanciful language.

WORKSHEET

Make an "X" in the space provided, if the sentence is written with fanciful language.

_(x)_ 1. Billowing clouds danced across the sky like waltzers dipping and turning.

_____ 2. Autumn colors touched the trees.

_____ 3. The bright eyes of the kitten peeped around the chair.

_(x)_ 4. Like tall soldiers at attention, the field of corn stood motionless in the afternoon sun.

_(x)_ 5. Light taps, like fingers drumming, rapped against the window. Steadily the rain came down.

_____ 6. The swimmers dove into the pool, quickly starting the race.

_(x)_ 7. Soft golden shadows bathed the quiet room where the children slept.

_(x)_ 8. Like a shining ribbon, the silver-streaked river curved and turned over the valley floor.

_____ 9. The mountains stood serene against the sky.

_____10. The force of the wind pushed the bending trees toward the ground.

Extended activity:

1. Have the students make a list of author use of fanciful language from various written sources—fiction work, travelogues, etc.
2. Have students rewrite newspaper accounts, using fanciful language techniques.

RECOGNIZING FANTASY AND REALITY

Objective: The students will demonstrate the ability to distinguish between fantasy and reality in written material by identifying elements which could or could not be possible.

Materials: given below

Procedure:

1. Give the students the prepared list of phrases.
2. The students are to place an "x" beside everything that they may read about in a story or book but would not be able to find anywhere on earth.
3. The students are to underline any phrase that refers to something or someone that could actually be found, seen, or heard on earth.
4. Discuss with students the reasons behind their choices, making sure they understand that they must be able to prove all things that are listed as real.

WORKSHEET

Read the following phrases. If it is a fantasy, something you would not find on earth, place an "x" in the blank before the phrase. If it is something real that you would find on earth, underline the phrase.

_____ a cat warming itself by the fire.
_(x)_ an ox as tall as a two-story building
_____ a telephone ringing off the wall
_(x)_ raining cats and dogs
_____ lightning flashes streaking across the sky
_____ a machine cutting out doughnuts
_____ a woman talking to herself

_(x)_   A green-bearded soldier watching rocket races
_(x)_   The Ghost of Christmas preseni
_____   mountains capped with snow
_____   a loud noise like thunder
_(x)_   a moon of green cheese

Evaluation: Check marked responses of the students.

Extended activities:

1. Have students compile a list of fantasy characters and real characters in books they are reading.
2. Have students compile lists of common sayings or phrases that have fantasy elements.

FACT OR OPINION—Lesson 1

Objective: Given statements of opinions and facts, students will distinguish between them.

Materials: a large number of written statements

Procedure:

1. Discuss the definition of fact and the definition of opinion, one being actual, the other unprovable.
2. Ask students which of these two statements is fact: (a) "Dogs make better pets than cats." (b) "There are more women than men in the United States." How can you prove it?
3. Have pupils number their papers from 1 to 10. Read these sentences or your own to them. Then write *F* for each statement of fact and *O* for each opinion.

    a. My brother will become President of the United States.

    b. The Great Smoky Mountains are prettier than the Rockies.

    c. Atlanta is the capital of Georgia.

    d. Breaking a mirror brings seven years of bad luck.

e. People from other countries are strange.

f. The most famous crops in Hawaii are sugar cane and pineapples.

g. In order to burn, a fire needs fuel and oxygen.

h. Boys have better manners than girls.

i. Pluto is the planet farthest from the sun.

j. English is more fun to study than arithmetic.

Talk about the statements and tell why you think they are facts or opinions.

Extended activities:

1. Have pupils write three statements of fact and three of opinion. Read your statements to the class, asking them to tell which are facts and which are opinions.
2. Have pupils listen carefully to the statements of other pupils in the class. As each statement is read, students should write whether it is a fact or an opinion. Use discussion of the statements to identify correct choices.

WORKSHEET—Lesson 1

Some of the following are facts and some are opinions. Think about each, then write the word *fact* or *opinion* after it. Give your reasons for calling some facts and others opinions. Note: Answers to fact questions should indicate that they are able to be *verified*.

a. The best tasting food in the world is hot apple pie. _____

REASON:

b. A deer is a four-legged animal. _____

REASON:

3. The best television story ever written is the one I saw last night.

_____

REASON:

d. Maple trees in the North lose their leaves in the winter. _____
REASON:

e. Basketball is the most exciting sport. _____
REASON:

f. There is a blanket of air all around the earth. _____
REASON:

g. There are 5,280 feet in a mile. _____
REASON:

FACT OR OPINION—Lesson 2

Objective: Students will be able to distinguish fact from opinion.

Materials: —several cards (any size) containing statements of fact
or opinion
—fact and opinion worksheet (see facing page)

Procedure:

1. Differentiate between fact and opinion by asking students for definitions and examples. Clear up their definitions, and give several sentences, asking the class which are factual and which are opinions.
2. Play fact/opinion card game by forming two teams. Show card to one team. Player on the team reads card and tells if it's a fact or opinion statement. If he answers correctly, his team scores a point. Give next card to next team.
3. Pass out worksheet to each student. Read over sheet with them. Students determine if article is completely true.
4. Students examine the article and cross out all opinion statements.

WORKSHEET—Lesson 2

Directions: Read the following article. Is everything in the article true? Is it a good article to send to a friend who wants to know more about Florida? *Your task is to underline all the opinion sentences.*

Florida is in the southeastern part of the United States. It is the most beautiful of our 50 states. Year round the weather is comfortable.

It is the safest place to be in winter. There are no snowy sidewalks to shovel or icy roads to drive.

People in Florida are very friendly. They are proud to have tourists visit their state.

Everyone who visits Orlando goes to Disney World. Disney World is a large tourist attraction.

Orange trees can be seen in many parts of the state. The growing of citrus fruits is a big business in Florida. Tourists do not leave Florida without seeing the orange groves.

Evaluation:

1. How well students play card game.
2. How well worksheet is completed.
3. Class discussion.

IDENTIFICATION OF PERSUASIVE TECHNIQUES

Objective: The student will identify propaganda techniques in written material by recognizing the author's intent to sway the reader to a particular point of view; by identifying the technique; or by identifying the elements of a particular technique.

Materials: —newspapers
—magazines
—political pamphlets

Procedure:

1. Identify the various types of techniques for the students:

   Bandwagon: the author implies that everyone is joining or presents a part of a particular view and suggests that you should join too.

   Testimonial: a well-known person endorses an item or viewpoint and recommends that you use or adopt the same.

   Transfer: if you use "X" product or believe "X" idea, then life will be better for you.

   Plain Folks: techniques in which the speaker or writer lists the "plain" background or similarities between the speaker and listeners and gives the impression that the listeners should support his ideas or views because they are just alike.

   Snob Appeal: appeals are directed to those who wish to think of themselves as part of a more select group.

   Scientific-Factual: use of scientific or factual information in a manner to support the view of a given person or group.

   Glittering Generalities: use of general terms that appeal to all and sound truthful and factual without being supported by substance or facts.

2. Discuss propaganda and ways in which it may be used; i.e., advertisements, political campaigns and pamphlets, civic campaigns and projects, editorials.

3. Have students look through magazines, newspapers, etc., to locate articles, advertisements, and editorials that demonstrate the types of propaganda techniques.

4. Have students write an advertisement for a product, either real or imaginary, that uses the propaganda techniques.

Evaluation:

Give students the prepared worksheet (opposite) which contains examples of propaganda techniques. Students are to match the type of propaganda technique to the statement.

WORKSHEET

A. Bandwagon
B. Testimonial
C Transfer
D. Glittering Generalities
E. Plain Folks
F. Snob Appeal
G. Scientific-Factual

1. _(G)_ Nine out of ten doctors surveyed recommend Sneezemore Cold medicine for their patients.
2. _(A)_ You too can be one of the millions of Americans enjoying Squiggle Bat, the newest water sport from Wetgamo. Buy yours today.
3. _(F)_ Only men of discriminating taste wear Hardsole Hiking Boots. Get yours today at Mr. Top's, the men's store in Appleville.
4. _(B)_ Hi, I'm Joe Slamo and I want to tell you about the best drink ever for ballplayers—Energyorange, the all-energy drink for ball players and all athletes.
5. _(C)_ Do you feel tired, left out of things, all alone? Would you like to be the center of attention at the next party you go to? Then use Glamor. Glamor, the newest shampoo from Dudso. Glamor can make you the hit of the party. Try it today!
6. _(E)_ I'm just a farmer like you folks. I know how much you worry about things going on in Washingotn today, and I promise you your concerns are my concerns.
7. _(D)_ All citizens for better schools will support the Better Schools Building Committee.

Extended activities:

1. Have students compile a classroom book of ads, editorials, and other sources that are examples of propaganda techniques.

2. Have students make a log of television and radio advertisements and the type of propaganda technique used in each.
3. Have students prepare, for a classroom election, campaign slogans and speeches that use different types of propaganda techniques.

RECOGNIZING AUTHOR'S PURPOSE

Objective: The students will demonstrate recognition of author purpose by identifying the purpose of a given selection.

Materials: —comic strips
—magazines
—newspapers
—books
—travel books

Procedure:

1. Begin with a teacher-led discussion. Ask the children if they know why an author writes. Proceed to answer their replies, and explain the four different purposes to the children. The four purposes are to inform, to entertain, to persuade, to describe. After explaining the four purposes to the children give them some examples of each, using material to demonstrate each one.
2. On the board, write five or six sentences using illustrations of the different types of author's purposes. Ask each student to label each sentence on a piece of paper. When all are finished, call on students to share their answers with the class, giving the reason that they chose the answer that they did.
3. Allow each child to view the different materials that you have brought in (the books, etc.). Give them a few minutes to browse, then tell them to select something short to present to the class, and to identify the author's purpose for writing that selection.
4. Pass out worksheet (see copy opposite). Have students complete it and turn it in.

WORKSHEET

UNDERSTANDING THE AUTHOR'S PURPOSE

Place in front of each sentence the word that best describes the primary purpose of that sentence.

INFORM   ENTERTAIN   DESCRIBE   PERSUADE

1. (describe) The silver 747 jet flew at great height and speed, leaving a trail of vapor behind it.
2. (persuade) Please go to the skating party because everyone else is going.
3. (entertain) John sat down in a bucket and ate his breakfast of sniggle berries smothered in orange gator-aide and topped with a chocolate bar.
4. (inform) The chess club will meet at 7 P.M. in the auditorium.
5. (inform) The winter schedule at the Resident Center will include BD426, on Tuesday, for all elementary education students.
6. (describe) The yellow petals surrounded the vibrant pink center on the flower standing alone among the green weeds.

Evaluation: Observe the students while they are presenting the materials that they chose to present and their reasons for the author's purpose.

Extended activities:

1. Have students write humorous stories and read them to the class.
2. Write a list of descriptive words on the board and have each student write a story using these words.
3. Describe a certain event to the class. Divide the class into four groups, and have each group write about the event from a different point of view, using the four different purposes as a viewpoint.
4. Make up a worksheet containing several short paragraphs. Ask the students to label each paragraph according to the author's purpose.

ALTERED SYNTAX

Objective: The student will identify the use of altered syntax as a technique of writing by rewriting sentences in altered syntax, and by identifying the sentences which have been altered.

Materials: given below

Procedure:

1. Have the students read the following sentences.

> The happy little girl licked the ice cream cone quickly.
> Happy, the little girl licked the ice cream cone quickly.
> The little happy girl licked the ice cream cone quickly.
> Quickly, the happy little girl licked the ice cream cone.
> The happy little girl licked quickly the ice cream cone.
>
> The young man walked down the street whistling.
> Whistling, the young man walked down the street.
> The young man, whistling, walked down the street.
> Down the street walked the whistling young man.
> Down the street walked the young man whistling.

2. Discuss with students what is different about each sentence. See if students can make the determination that all sentences in each example contain exactly the same words but words are arranged differently.
3. Discuss reasons for author use of altered syntax: variety of sentences, more interesting, to create special effects.
4. Ask students to choose the most interesting sentences (answers will vary), or to decide if some examples are more interesting than others.
5. Give students sentences and have them reconstruct in altered syntax.

> The train chugged slowly up the hill.
> John has only five dollars.

Evaluation:

Check the sets of sentences that students have rewritten. Prepare a list of sentences that contain sentences written in regular form and in altered syntax form. The student is to choose the altered syntax form. (Given on facing page.)

WORKSHEET

You are to read the sentence pairs below. Mark an "X" in the space before the sentence written in altered form.

___ Mary left the room walking softly.
_(x)_ Walking softly, Mary left the room.

___ The parade marched noisily down the street.
_(x)_ Noisily, the parade marched down the sstreet.

_(x)_ As the clouds gathered and the wind began to howl, the campers huddled in their tent.
___ The campers huddled in their tent as the clouds gathered and the wind began to howl.

___ Many children collected pennies to help make the Red Cross Drive successful.
_(x)_ To help make the Red Cross Drive successful, many children collected pennies.

_(x)_ Jumping and running excitedly, the dogs leaped across the fence.
___ The jumping and running dogs leaped excitedly across the fence.

Extended activities:

1. Have students find sentences in written material which have altered syntax.
2. Have students write expressions of dialects that they have heard or are familiar with which are examples of altered syntax. Examples may be Pennsylvania Dutch, Louisiana Cajun, foreign expressions in which sentence structure differs from English language.

SYMBOLS

Objective: Given a symbol, the student will identify it, or select the meaning of a given symbol, or choose the best symbol for a trait or concept.

Materials: —a set of symbols including a set of international traffic signs.
—a justice scale

—a poison symbol
—a peace sign
—a medical symbol
—a four-leaf clover, etc.

Procedure:

1. Show the students a familiar symbol such as a mathematical operations sign, a plus sign, an equals sign, etc., and ask them if they know what that symbol represents. Explain to the students that there are many symbols in everyday life that they can read and use very frequently.
2. Show other examples of symbols and have students identify them.
3. Ask the students to name other symbols that are used frequently.
4. Have students make a list of symbols and their meanings.

Evaluation: Give the students a prepared sheet of symbols. They are to match the written definition with the correct symbol.

Extended activity:

1. Have students make posterboard symbols for the classroom.
2. Have students design and make symbol cards for specific classroom use, such as a symbol for a sharing area, art area, etc.
3. Give the students an ideal or concept and have them supply a symbol.

SYMBOLISM

Objective: The students will demonstrate recognition of author use of symbolism by identifying the symbol used, and by defining the symbolism and meaning in their own terms.

Materials: copies of "No Man Is an Island" written by John Donne (on facing page)

Procedure:

1. Introduce to students the concept that authors often use symbols to convey a meaning or ideal that they wish the reader to understand.
2. Have students read the poem "No Man Is an Island."
3. The students are to identify the symbol used by Donne and discuss how he used it to make a statement about man and his environment.
4. Have students work through questions below, either orally or as a written exercise.

WORKSHEET
NO MAN IS AN ISLAND*

No man is an island, entire of itself;
Every man is a piece of the continent, a part of the main;
If a clod be washed away by the sea, Europe is the less,
As well as if a promontory were, as well as if a manor
Of thy friends or of thine own were;
Any man's death diminishes me, because I am involved in mankind;
And therefore never send to know for whom the bell tolls;
It tolls for thee.

John Donne

*Postman, Neil, *Language and Reality*. Holt, Rhinehart and Winston, Inc., New York, 1966. p. 295.

1. The author uses symbols to make a statement about man in this poem. What are the symbols he uses? (Island, piece of the continent, a clod.)
2. What meaning is the author trying to convey when he states, "No man is an island, entire of self; Every man is a piece of the continent, a part of the main"? (Man does not live alone, he must help and be helped by others.)
3. What is the symbolic meaning behind the following lines: "If a clod be washed away by the sea, Europe is the less, As well as if a promontory were, as well as if a manor of thy friends or of thine own were"? (The loss of some part of mankind is a loss for all mankind.)
4. What is the meaning of the phrase, "And therefore never send to know for whom the bell tolls; It tolls for thee"? (Never worry about death because death will come to all.)

Evaluation: Rate students' oral discussion of poem or check worksheet answers.

Extended activities:

1. Have students make a list of things that may be used symboli-
cally to present an idea or thought.

> sun—life
> flag—country, patriotism
> still water—deepness, thoughtfulness
> (still waters run deep.)
> fire—light, warmth, destroyer
> mountains—steadfastness, endurance, strength
> valley—protection, shelter, prison, confining

2. Have students make up or name known symbols or behavior that
symbolizes the following:

happiness	respect for others
peace	conformity
love of mankind	patriotism
love of self	wealth

Brief Review–Critical Comprehension Skills

Upon reaching this point, you have either read the critical reading skill lessons or you have used them with your students. In either
case, you have seen that this chapter can be used to develop skills
that you have perhaps not seen in the reading program available to
you and your colleagues. This is all the more reason for you to make
vigorous use of these plans so that your students will not be
shortchanged in their critical reading skill development. Only you,
the teacher, can think, plan, and teach what is needed. No program
or group of lessons can substitute for you. So use your judgment and
wisely formulate a strategy for using the critical reading lesson plans
in this chapter not just once, but again and again as needed. By
doing this, you will be the thinking, discriminating professional
who prescriptively meets student needs.

9
Modern Approach to Study Skills

By placing study skill lessons in the last chapter, we are not implying that they are any less valuable than any other set of skills. On the contrary—study skills are becoming recognized more frequently than ever as having a cause and effect relationship to the global skill we call reading. What literacy test exists that does not assess some of these skills?

We, like you, have usually taught these skills by referring our students to particular areas of the book we were intending to teach. If you do that, have you noticed that students easily drift away from the glossary or whichever section you are dealing with? If you have, then we have a suggestion for you, and it is this: put your illustration on a transparency and project it on an overhead projector. (You may want to do that with the illustrated figures in this chapter.) All eyes will be focused on the screen. You will have drift-free attention for explaining what you want your students to learn. After you have accomplished your mission, then you can use the books for realistic instruction. We believe this suggestion will increase your effectiveness as you provide additional reinforcement.

TABLE OF CONTENTS

Objective: The student will be able to understand and use the table of contents of any book through analysis of its contents.

Materials: a table of contents, whether from a classroom textbook or a teacher-prepared table of contents

Procedure:

1. Show the students the table of contents.
2. Discuss where in the book the table of contents is found and its purpose.
3. Ask specific questions that require analysis of the table of contents.

Example:

TABLE OF CONTENTS

Unit One: THE SEACOAST

Stranded on Salmon Island   3
Fisherman Dependency................................   8
Fishing in the South......................................   12

Unit Two: THE JUNGLE

Step into the Jungle..   19
The Trader of the Congo   22
Trading in the Market................................   30
The Fascinating Jungle................................   38

Unit Three: THE DESERT

Life in the Desert..   45
The Sahara Desert   51
The Desert Animals   60

Unit Four: GAMES

The Problem with Games...........................   70
Games to Make   76
Games for all Ages   86

Unit Five: MATHEMATICS

Reading about Numbers...............................   90
Working with Math Words.............................   100
Figures for All Occasions.............................   107
How Much and How Many   111

Questions:

1. How many units are in the book? (5)
2. Are all the units about the same subject? (No)
3. How many units have the same number of stories in them? (Units One, Three and Four with three stories, and Units Two and Five with four.)
4. Are the units in alphabetical order? (No.) Why or why not? (Answers will vary).
5. What subject does Unit Five deal with? (Mathematics)
6. Why do you think each unit is given a title? (Answers will vary.)
7. In Unit Three, on what page does the story "The Sahara Desert" begin? (51) End? (59)
8. Why does "The Sahara Desert" not end on page 60? (That is the first page of the story "The Desert Animals.")
9. What story describes something to make? ("Games to Make.")
10. What story might help you if you were having a problem understanding mathematical words? ("Working with Math Words.")
11. On what page would you look to find out about:
    a) The desert animals (60)
    b) Fishing in the south (12)
    c) Mathematical figures (107)
12. If you needed to know about trading in the jungle, where would you look? (Pages 22 and 30.)
13. Which unit is the shortest? (Unit One)
14. How many pages are in Unit Three? (24)
15. Why is a Table of Contents necessary? (Answers will vary.)
16. Looking at this Table of Contents, which unit would you be most interested in reading? (Answers will vary.)

Extended activities:

1. Use textbooks and have students make questions about the table of contents for other students.
2. Have prepared riddle-type questions relating to a table of contents, such as, "I can tell about snakes in Florida. Which unit am I?" "Three of us are the same length. What chapters are we?"
3. Take several content pages from discarded books. Cut apart the titles, authors' names, and page numbers. Have students in a group arrange the parts under the headings of *who, what, where*. After the table of contents is cut apart, have the students draw

from each heading and write a creative story using the parts
drawn.
4. Have students write a creative story, adding a table of contents as
a cover page.

USING THE INDEX

Objective: The student will be able to use the index through active
participation in analyzing its contents.

Materials: the index in a textbook

Procedure:

1. Guide students to the index section of the book.
2. Discuss the format of the index, comparing it to the other sections of the book, such as the table of contents and the glossary.
3. Lead the discussion on the function of the index.

Example:

INDEX

Addend, 11, 20, 82
Adding
  fractions, 230
  hundreds, 32
  sums of ten, 111
  three numbers, 37, 42, 86
Addition, 10, 36
  associative property, 37, 42, 90
  communitative property, 12, 16, 37
  on a number line, 29-30, 48, 102
  renaming, 36-37, 82, 221
  using two-digit numerals, 81, 86, 90, 101, 118
Angle, 224, 226

Area, 248, 353, 384
Calendar, 246
Cent, 129, 227
Centimeter, 295
Circle, 244, 286, 384
Diameter, 248, 250
Estimating
  area, 113
  a product, 220, 333
  a quotient, 200-203
Factor, 99, 339
  greater than ten, 261
  unnamed, 149, 155, 201, 203, 233, 346
  zero as a, 106, 350

Questions:

1. Are the words in alphabetical order? (Yes.)
2. Look at the word *addition*. Are the skills under addition in alphabetical order? (Yes.)
3. Why is it important to put the words in alphabetical order? (To be able to find things quickly.)
4. How is the index different from the glossary? (The glossary gives the meaning of the word and the index gives the page numbers on which the word is found.)
5. Do you have to know the meaning of the word to find it in the index? (No.)
6. On what page would you find information about centimeters? (Page 295.)
7. How many skills are listed under *Addition*? (5)
8. Look under *Addition* for "on a number line." There is a dash between 29-30. What does the dash mean? (The subject begins on page 29 and continues to page 30.)
9. What does the comma between the numbers mean? (The information is only on the page(s) given and does not continue to the following page listed.)
10. How many pages deal with the subject of area? (3) What are the page numbers? (248, 353, 384)
11. What subject is discussed on page 246? (Calendar.)
12. If you needed information on renaming in addition, on what page would you look? (Pages 36-37, 82, 221.)

Extended activities:

1. Have small groups of students make an index for a short story or short newspaper article.
2. Have individuals or small groups of students write their own story from an index.

SUMMARIZING

Objective: The student will be able to apply the skill of summarizing to ideas seen, heard, or presented in written material.

Materials: several short paragraphs; several pictures

Procedure:

1. Explain to the students what is meant by summarizing and the value of being able to summarize.
2. Read a short paragraph to the students. When finished, give several statements, then ask them to choose which one statement summarizes the paragraph.
3. Repeat step 2, using several paragraphs.
4. Next read a short passage and have students give a one-sentence summation of the passage.
5. Show students a picture and have a summation given of the picture.
6. Repeat step 5 until students are successful in giving one-sentence summations.

Extended activities:

1. Show students a film or filmstrip without the sound. Have them summarize what was seen.
2. Have students illustrate the main point of a story.
3. Have students rewrite a story to a shorter form.
4. Assign homework of watching a certain T.V. program. The students then have a certain amount of time in which to tell the class about the program.
5. Show the students a film or video tape of a sport being played, then have them summarize the events of the game.
6. Summarize and have students list at least two events under each heading.

Example: A. The American People
         1.
         2.
       B. World War I
         1.
         2.
       C. America
         1.
         2.

OUTLINING

Objective: The student will be able to outline the main events of written materials.

Materials: newspaper article

Procedure:

1. Read a newspaper article to the students.
2. Explain that together you are going to outline the article, explaining that outlining an article means analyzing the contents.
3. Discuss the value of knowing how to outline.
4. Draw an inverted pyramid on the chalkboard:

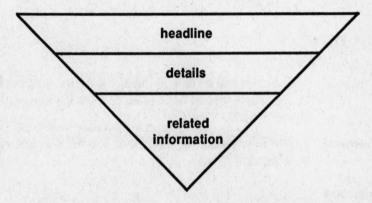

5. Discuss the shape of the pyramid, helping students to discover the degrees of importance given each heading.
6. Reread the article, asking the students to listen so that together you can fill in the pyramid.
7. Reconstruct the pyramid as follows:

   I. (Headline)
     A. (Details)
     B.
       1. (Related Information)
       2.

8. Through discussion, fill in the outline with information gained from the newspaper article.

Extended activities:

1. Distribute other articles and have students, working in pairs or small groups, outline the article.
2. Have individuals or small groups of students create an outline of something of interest. The groups or individuals exchange outlines and write a story from it.
3. After reading a short passage, give the students an outline in scrambled order. They rearrange the outline into its correct form. The passage read should be available for the students to work with while unscrambling the outline.

SKIMMING:

Objective: The student will be able to quickly skim the material to be read for a general impression of what the material is about.

Materials: a newspaper article or a textbook chapter that has not been previously read

Procedure:

1. Discuss the purpose of skimming material before it is read.
2. Explain that skimming is systematic and organized.
3. Refer to newspaper article or a textbook and ask students:

    a) What is the title? (and subtitle, if any?)
    b) Read the first couple of sentences in the selection.
    c) Read any subtitles and first couple of sentences.
    d) Read the last two or three sentences.

4. Have an open discussion on what the students think they will read about when reading the material completely.
5. Ask for student reactions on the worth of skimming material.

Extended activities:

1. Have prepared questions on short articles that a student could answer by skimming.
2. Ask a question and time the response.
3. From an article, have students mark in different colors all the words that would fit in the categories: who, what, why, when, where. The students can then write their own stories from the words from the five categories.

SCANNING

Objective: By answering questions related to an advertisement, students will demonstrate their ability to locate information.

Materials: ads from the local newspaper or a magazine

Procedure:

1. Display an ad from the newspaper or magazine. (Opaque projector is most useful.)
2. Discuss the ad with the students: where would you find the ad, type of ad, purpose of ads, etc.
3. Ask specific questions which require scanning the ad for answers. Show students copies of the boxed ad beginning "Come on in" (page 226) and ask the following questions:

WORKSHEET

1) Where is Tom Peely Chevrolet located?
   (897 East Commercial Street, Tucktown, New York)
2) Is the telephone number given? (Yes.)
3) How many Camaros are listed? (5) Monte Carlos (3)
4) Which car is the most expensive? (1976 Landau Coupe.)
   Least Expensive? (1971 Monte Carlo Coupe.)
5) Which model year has the most cars listed? (1974)

6) How many cars are blue? (2)
7) Which cars have air conditioning? (First, fourth, fifth, sixth, seventh, eighth.)
8) Which car has the most features? (Last one.)
9) What is the stock number of the least expensive car? (#8111)
10) Which car would you buy? Why?

COME ON IN !!!

Camaros

1974 Type LT Stock #1234, Dark Blue metallic, cloth interior, rally wheels, air, console, automatic, low miles. $4595

1972 Sport Coupe Stock #283, Bright Green with Green Vinyl interior, economical 6 cylinder with 3 speed, Cragar wheels.
$2798

1976 Sport Coupe Stock #6789, Bright Red with sport cloth seating, 3 speed and 6 cylinder $3195

1971 Rally Sport Stock #887, Burnt Orange, White vinyl top and interior, console, air, automatic. $2795

1974 Type LT Stock #9876, Light Blue, Black vinyl top and custom interior, air, console, automatic. $4155

Monte Carlos

1971 Coupe Stock #8111, tan color with cream vinyl top, cloth interior, air, automatic. $2595

1974 "S" Coupe Stock #4564, Red, Saddle vinyl top, Saddle buckets, console, air, automatic, new tires.
$3850

1976 Landau Coupe Stock #3212, Firethorn with white vinyl top, white buckets, console, air, automatic, tilt wheel, cruise control, stereo power windows and door locks. $5495

TOM PEELY CHEVROLET
897 East Commercial Street
Tucktown, New York 37773
(305) 888-9990

Extended activity:

Have other ads and questions prepared for students to work independently. For example, see the ad on page 228.

WORKSHEET

1. What type of ad is this?
2. Where would you buy these tires? (Mike's)
3. How many general types of tires are there? (3—nylon, belted, radial.)
4. How many models listed would the compact tires fit? (11)
5. What size tire would you buy for an Olds 88? (H78-15)
6. How much difference in price is there between a nylon blackwall and a belted radial for a Fury? Include the F.E.T. ($11.19)
7. Which tires are the most expensive? (H78-15 & L78-15) Least expensive? (A78-13)
8. Are the cars listed in alphabetical order? (No.)
9. Why are the blackwalls less expensive than the whitewalls? (Cost less to produce.)
10. Which would you buy? Why?

USING THE GLOSSARY

Objective: The students will be able to understand and use a glossary through active participation of analyzing its contents.

Materials: a glossary from a classroom textbook

Procedure:

1. Direct students to the glossary in a textbook.
2. Discuss the purpose and use of the glossary.
3. Have students examine the contents of the glossary by asking questions about the words in the glossary.

MIKE'S TIRES	For most models of:	Size	Nylon Black-Walls	Plus F.E.T.	Belted White-walls	Plus F.E.T.	Radial White-walls	Plus F.E.T.
Sub-Compacts	Vega, Capri, Datsun, Pinto, Skyhawk, Monza, Mustang II, Volkswagon, Fiat	A78-13 B78-13 560-15	16.50 18.50 20.50	1.72 1.82 1.77	28.88	2.01	36.00 38.00	1.84 2.00
Compacts	Hornet, Gremlin, Dart, Maverick, Javelin, Granada, Comet, Nova, Camaro, Coronet, Omega	C78-14 D78-14 E78-14	20.50 21.00 22.00	2.01 2.23 2.37	29.88	2.09	38.00 34.00 43.00	2.27 2.41 2.54
Mid-Size	Matador, Fury, Chevelle, Cordoba, Charger, Cutlass	G78-14 H78-14 G78-15	24.00 24.00 24.00	2.49 2.53 2.59	34.88	2.80	45.00 48.00 46.00	2.69 2.81 2.79
Full-Size	Impala, Caprice, Olds 88, Cadillac, Lincoln, Ford/ GM Wagons	H78-15 L78-15	26.00 26.00	2.79 2.79	36.88	3.12	49.00 51.00	2.96 3.28

Example:

GLOSSARY

able—a ble: having the power to do something.

admire—ad mire: to look at with pleasure.

aircraft—air craft: an object that will fly or float in the air.

boomerang—boom er ang: a curved piece of wood that can be thrown so it will return.

boundary—bound a ry: an edge that shows the end of something.

calendar—cal en dar: a chart that shows the day, month, and year.

certain—cer tain: without any doubt; sure.

clean—free from dirt.

clerk—(1) a person who works in a store selling things; (2) a person who works in an office.

detective—de tec tive: a person who solves mysteries by getting facts.

diamond—di a mond: (1) a valuable stone; (2) the shape of a baseball field; (3) a figure.

diplomacy — di plo ma cy: tact; skill in getting along with people.

Questions:

1. How many words begin with a? (3)
2. Are they in alphabetical order? (Yes.)
3. Why is it important that they are listed alphabetically? (To be able to find them quickly.)
4. In the story "Australia" you will find the word *boomerang*. Using the glossary, what does *boomerang* mean? (A curved piece of wood that can be thrown so it will come back.)
5. Why are some words written several ways? (Shows the number of syllables? in the word.)
6. How many words are one syllable? (2); two syllables? (4); three syllables ? (5); four syllables? (1).
7. How many meanings does the word *diamond* have? (3)
8. What other word has more than one meaning? (Clerk.)
9. Looking at the meanings of the word *clerk,* what do they have in common? (Both are working people.)
10. What other book is the glossary like? (Dictionary.)

11. If you have a dictionary, why would this book need a glossary?
(The glossary has only words from this book, where a dictionary
has all words.)

Extended activities:

1. Have prepared questions using other glossaries or teacher-prepared glossaries that students answer independently or in small
groups.
2. Have small groups create a glossary for a special topic. These
can be special interest topics, a TV program, school subject, etc.
They write each word with its pronunciation and definition on a
separate index card for alphabetizing purposes. The glossary is
then developed from the index cards.
3. Stories, speeches, books can be created by using the glossary
developed in Activity 2.
4. A game-type quiz can be made by asking such questions as:

1) What is a three-syllable word that means "the edge that
shows the end of something"? (Boundary.)
2) What word beginning with "*c*" means "free from dirt"?
(Clean.)

INTERPRETING GRAPHIC MATERIALS

Objective: To provide instruction in reading and interpreting data
given on graphs.

Materials: three graphs: bar, line, picture

Procedure:

(Note: Students should begin developing skills in reading
graphs at a basic level and graduate to a more complex
level.)

1. Show the students one of the graphs. (The order used for introduction of the graph—line, bar, or picture—will depend on the
simplicity of the graph.)
2. Ask specific questions about the graph.

Example: Bar graph

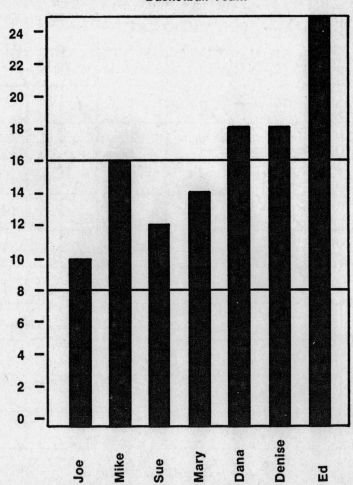

Basketball Team

1. What does this graph show? (Individual basketball scores.)
2. Who made the most points? (Ed.)
3. Did anyone score the same? (Yes.) Who? (Dana and Denise.)
4. Who scored more, Joe or Sue? (Sue.)
5. How many players are shown on the graph? (7)
6. How would you show 11 points on the graph? (Draw bar halfway between 10 and 12.)

Example: Line graph

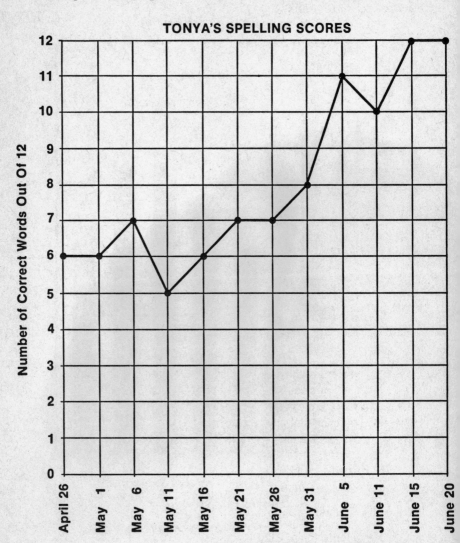

TONYA'S SPELLING SCORES

1. What is the purpose of this graph? (To show Tonya's spelling scores.)
2. On what date did Tonya get the least correct? (May 11.) The most correct? (June 15 and 20.)

3. How many times did Tonya's score drop? (Twice.) On what dates did the scores drop? (May 11 and June 11.)
4. On what dates did Tonya make the same score? (April 26, May 1, and May 16; May 6, May 21, and May 26; June 15 and June 20.)

Example: Picture graph

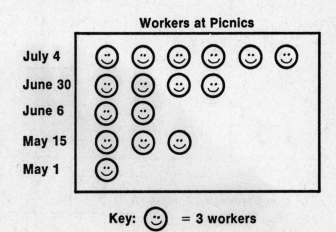

Workers at Picnics

Key: ☺ = 3 workers

1. What is the name of the graph? (Workers at Picnics.)
2. How many workers does 1 ☺ equal? (3)
3. What day had the most workers? (July 4.)
4. Why do you think that day had the most workers? (Answers will vary, but the fact that July 4 is a national holiday should be mentioned.)
5. Which day had 12 workers? (June 30)
6. How many workers were at the picnic on May 15? (9)

Extended activities:

1. Have students make their own graphs. Small groups can make graphs of different characteristics of the group, such as height, weight, color of eyes, favorite television shows, number of books read during a span of time.
2. Bulletin board to show pupils' progress in a certain area. (see example on following page.)

(BULLETIN BOARD)
My Progress in Recall of Math Facts

	1	2	3	4
Tim	3 min. 43 sec.			
Carol	4 min. 3 sec.			
Bill	3 min. ☺			
Mary	3 min. 20 sec.			

Give students 100 basic math facts. Time their work. Record time. Place the happy face when there is 100% accuracy on the recall of the math facts tested in the least amount of time.

3. Show pupils a graph and ask True and False questions about the graph.

READING MAPS

Objective: To provide instruction in reading and understanding the details of a map.

Materials: a map (dittoed or on a overhead projector)

Procedure:

1. Show students the picture of the map.
2. Ask questions specific to the map provided (see example). Be sure to include questions that start basically and graduate to reason.

   1. What is the title of the map? (University of Central Florida.)

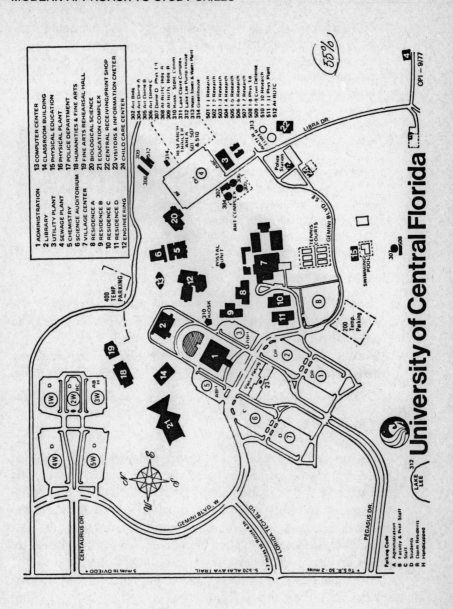

University of Central Florida

2. How are the buildings on the map represented? (With numbers.)
3. Do all the numbers on the map represent buildings? (No.)
4. How can you tell the difference? (The numbers for the buildings are printed in black blocks.)
5. Would you know how large the campus is? Why or why not? (Answers may vary—but call attention to the fact that no scale is provided.)
6. What are the numbers of the buildings in which the students live? (8, 9, 10, 11)
7. What do the black numbers in the circles indicate? (Parking lots.)
8. To what building would you go if you were a visitor and needed information? (#23—Visitors and Information Center.)
9. Where do you think north campus is? (Answers will vary.)
10. Would you have difficulty using this map if you had never been on this campus before? Why or why not? (Answers will vary.)

Extended activities:

1. Have students locate maps and write questions concerning them. They can exchange questions and maps. This can be done independently or as a group.
2. Students could create original maps and have others evaluate their validity and usefulness by making up questions based on the map.

Brief Review–Study Skills

Given the fact that these study skills cannot be totally acquired by all your students under the best of instructional conditions, we do think these lesson plans provide you with a nucleus for a substantial start on these skills. And besides moving from these lessons into book material, with some alterations such as developing alternate transparencies, these basic plans can provide you with valuable resources for effectively nailing down these skills with your students.

We think it is well worth noting that our instruction as teachers provides skill development for our students so they will be able to continue a lifetime of learning. In school or out of school, a person's ability to use study skills is vital. There is no substitute for being an independent learner. These skills further this goal.

Index

A

Ability to make judgments, 194
Actions, character analysis related to character, 173
Adjectival recognition, 113
Affixes—prefixes, 108
Affixes—suffixes, 108
Agreement with subject, verbs, 123
Alphabet knowledge, 38
Altered syntax, 210
Analysis, related to character actions, 173
Antonyms, 48, 49
Antonyms, recognizing in context, 66
Application, initial consonants (single), 76
Auditory discrimination, 22
Auditory, initial consonants (single), 74
Auditory memory, 23
Author's purpose, recognizing, 208

B

Blending word elements, 96, 97
Blends, consonant (association and application), 80
Blends, consonant (other), 82
Blends, consonant (r-blends), 81
Blends, consonant (visual-auditory), 79
Book, parts of (glossary), 227
Book, parts of (index), 220
Book, parts of (table of contents), 217

C

Cause and effect relationships, 160
Character analysis related to character actions, 173

Character feelings, 171

Character feelings, 171
Clues, context, using, 59, 61, 62
Combinations, vowel sounds, 92
Compound words, 118
Conclusions, drawing, 163
Consonant digraphs, 87
Consonant blends (association and application), 80
Consonant blends (other), 82
Consonant blends (r-blends), 81
Consonant blends (visual-auditory), 79
Consonants, ending, 77
Consonants, initial (single)—auditory, 74
Consonants, initial (single)—application, 76
Consonants, initial (single)—visual, 75
Context, antonyms in, 66
Context clues, using, 59, 61, 62
Context, homographs in, 68
Context, homophones in, 63
Contractions, 117
Copying words, 39

D

Details, recalling (action words), 155
Details, recalling (*how* words), 150
Details, recalling (*when* words), 153
Details, recalling (*where* words), 152
Details, recalling (*who/what* words), 154
Details, recalling (*why* words), 151
Development, motor (body control), 29
Development, motor (eye-hand control), 31
Development, motor (left-to-right orientation), 34
Development, motor (oral language development, 32
Development, motor (sequence pictures), 35

Digraphs, consonant, 87
Discrimination, auditory, 22
Discrimination, visual, 25
Distinguishing between nouns and verbs, 125
Drawing conclusions, 163
Drawing inferences, prediction of future action by, 165

E

Employment and recognition of idioms and figurative language, 179
Ending consonants, 77
Endings, inflected (ed), 106
Endings, inflected (ing), 107
Endings, inflected (s), 103
Endings, inflected (singular/plural), 105
Expressions, figurative, 180

F

Fables, recognition of, 195
Fact or opinion, 202, 204
Fanciful language, recognition of, 199
Fantasy and reality, recognition of, 201
Feelings, character, 171
Figurative expressions, 180
Figurative language, recognition and employment of idioms and, 179
Future action, prediction of by drawing inference, 165

G

Glossary, using, 227
Graphic materials, interpreting, 230

H

Heteronyms, 52
Homographs in context, 68
Homonyms, 50
Homophones in context, 63

I

Idea, main (details), 168
Idea, main (paragraphs), 169

Idea, main (titles), 165
Identification of persuasive techniques, 205
Identification of sentence parts, 129
Idioms and figurative language, recognition and employment of, 179
Index, using, 220
Inference, perception of, 161
Inflected word ending (ed), 106
Inflected word ending (ing), 107
Inflected word ending (s), 103
Inflected words (singular/plural), 105
Initial consonants (single)—application, 76
Initial consonants (single)—auditory, 74
Initial consonants (single)—visual, 75
Interpreting graphic materials, 230
Irony, recognition of, 198
Irregular agreement with subject, verbs, 123

J

Judgments, ability to make, 194

K

Knowledge, alphabet, 38

L

Language, figurative, recognition and employment of idioms and, 179
Left-to-right orientation, 34
Letters, silent in words, 98
Listening, 28
Long and short vowels, 89
Long vowel sounds, 88

M

Main idea (details), 168
Main idea (paragraphs), 169
Main idea (titles), 165
Maps, reading, 234
Meaning, phrase, 127
Meanings, multiple, 54
Memory, auditory, 23
Memory, visual, 26
Metaphors and similes, 181
Mood, perception of, 185
Motor development (body control), 29

Motor development (eye-hand control), 31
Motor development (oral language development), 32
Motor development (sequence pictures), 35
Multiple meanings, 54
Myths, recognition of, 197

N

Nouns and verbs, distinguishing between, 125
Number of syllables (audio-visual), 133

O

Opinion, fact or, 202, 204
Outlining, 223

P

Parts of a book (glossary), 227
Parts of a book (index), 220
Parts of a book (table of contents), 217
Perception of imagery, 58
Perception of inference, 161
Perception of mood, 185
Perception of sensory imagery, 176
Period, time, 186
Persuasive techniques, identification of, 205
Phrase meaning, 127
Phrases, prepositional, 114
Pictured material, reading graphs, 230
Plural form, possessives, 111
Possessives, plural form, 111
Possessives, singular form, 109
Prediction of future action by drawing inferences, 165
Prepositional phrases, 114
Principle, VCCV, 134
Principle, VCV, 135
Printed material, reading (scanning), 225
Printed material, reading (skimming), 224
Pronouns, 115
Punctuation: scrambled sentences, 130
Purpose, recognizing author's, 208

Q

Quotations, 131

R

R-controlled vowel sounds, 91
Reading pictured material (graphs), 230
Reading pictured material (maps), 234
Reading printed material (scanning), 225
Reading printed material (skimming), 224
Recalling details (action words), 155
Recalling details (*how* words), 150
Recalling details (*when* words), 153
Recalling details (*where* words), 152
Recalling details (*who/what* words), 154
Recalling details (*why* words), 151
Recognition, adjectival, 113
Recognition and employment of idioms and figurative language, 179
Recognition of fables, 195
Recognition of fanciful language, 199
Recognition of fantasy and reality, 201
Recognition of irony, 198
Recognition of myths, 197
Recognition of satire, 196
Recognizing antonyms in context, 66
Recognizing author's purpose, 208
Relationship, cause and effect, 160
Rhyming words, 93, 95
Root words, 122

S

Satire, recognition of, 196
Scanning, 225
Scrambled sentences, punctuation, 130
Selecting correct synonyms, 64
Sensible sequence, 141
Sensory imagery, perception of, 176
Sentence parts, identification of, 129
Sentences scrambled, punctuation, 130
Sequence of events—parts, 143
Sequence pictures (motor development), 35
Sequence (sensible sequence—pictures), understanding, 141
Sequence (understanding events or parts), 143
Sequence (understanding story events), 145
Sequential order of events, 36
Setting, story, 148
Sight vocabulary, 53
Silent letters in words, 98

Silent vowel sounds, 90
Similes and metaphors, 181
Singular form, possessives, 109
Scanning, reading printed material, 225
Short vowel sounds, 87
Skimming, reading printed material, 224
Sounds, vowel (combinations), 92
Sounds, vowel (long), 88
Sounds, vowel (long and short), 89
Sounds, vowel (r-controlled), 91
Sounds, vowel (short), 87
Sounds, vowel (silent), 90
Story setting, 148
Subject, irregular agreement with verbs, 123
Suffixes, 108
Summarizing, 221
Syllables and vowel principles, 136
Syllables, number of (audio-visual), 133
Symbolism, 212
Symbols, 211
Synonyms, 43
Synonyms, selecting correct, 64
Syntax, altered, 210

T

Table of contents, 217
Techniques, persuasive, identification of, 205
Tense usage, verbs, 124
Time period, 186

U

Understanding sequence of events (story), 145

Understanding sequence (sensible sequence—pictures), 141
Understanding sequence (sequence of events or parts), 143
Using context clues, 59, 61, 62
Using the glossary, 227
Using the index, 220

V

Verbs and nouns, distinguishing between, 125
Verbs, irregular agreement with subject, 123
Verbs, tense usage, 124
VCCV principle, 134
VCV principle, 135
Visual discrimination, 25
Visual, initial consonants (single), 75
Visual memory, 26
Vocabulary, sight, 53
Vowel principles and syllables, 136
Vowel sounds (long), 88
Vowel sounds (long and short), 89
Vowel sounds (r-controlled), 91
Vowel sounds (short), 87
Vowel sounds (silent), 90
Vowel sounds (combinations), 92

W

Word elements, blending, 96, 97
Words, compound, 118
Words, copying, 39
Words, rhyming, 93
Words root, 122
Words, silent letters in, 98